The Presentation Play

PHILIPPE DE MÉZIÈRES

Figurative Representation of the Presentation of the Virgin Mary in the Temple

Translated and edited by Robert S. Haller
Introduction by M. Catherine Rupp, O.S.M.

UNIVERSITY OF NEBRASKA PRESS · LINCOLN

The Latin texts used in this book are taken from
The Drama of the Medieval Church by Karl Young,
by permission of the Clarendon Press, Oxford.

Publishers on the Plains
UNP

Copyright © 1971 by the University of Nebraska Press

All rights reserved

International Standard Book Number 0–8032–0780–8

Library of Congress Catalog Card Number 71–125315

Manufactured in the United States of America

Contents

v

Preface

In recent years, there has justifiably been great interest in the aesthetics which lie behind the monumental literary works of the late Middle Ages. Since these works were produced by men like Dante and Petrarch, Eustace Deschamps and Oton de Graunson, Henry Duke of Lancaster and Geoffrey Chaucer, who combined careers as diplomats and soldiers with the writing of elaborate and learned poetry and prose, they have a natural autobiographic interest. But many such works are so tenuously connected with the life of their authors that the motive for their having been written can be discovered only by the exploration of the kind of symbolic or allegorical imagination which, to these writers, gave moral grandeur to their works as to their lives. Fictions which are made meaningful on several complementary allegorical levels—moral, doctrinal, and cosmic—are also applicable to the larger problems of political and personal life. The large symbols in these works, the pilgrimages, dream visions, mirrors, parliaments, battles, and triumphs with which they are filled, were facts of life as well as metaphors for divine and human purposefulness. The man of letters who was also man of action united his life and related his learning to practical problems by absorbing and practicing the interpretative methods of late medieval humanistic theology.

This translation of Philippe de Mézières' Presentation Play has as its purpose to make more widely available a key document in fourteenth-century aesthetics. Its author was also a political and a literary figure of no small importance. The formality and self-depreciation of his style, set off as they are by his moral refinement and piety and by his wide reading and experience of the world, have much in common with the qualities of other fourteenth-century prose works written by men of affairs. Most of Philippe's literary efforts support his political purposes in reflecting his advocacy of the Crusades and his devotion to peace among European powers and to the spiritual renewal of European knighthood. And even a work like the Presentation Play, which seems at first glance more devotional than political, can in fact be best understood as an exercise in cosmic diplomacy. In honoring the Virgin and in recalling the foundations of the Christian faith, a Christian congregation is also engaging in a rite in which they acknowledge their common allegiance and obligations.

It is easy for us to assume that plays have always served the same function in all societies, or to assume that this function is so obvious in the content of plays as to require no explanation. But Philippe de Mézières did not believe that his play could stand on its own without the most detailed exposition of both the motivation of its performance and the elements of its production. About the motivation of other medieval plays we know very little. Their authors are anonymous and, although we know that, for instance, the cycle plays were performed on wagons at the feast of Corpus Christi, or the *quem quaeritis* tropes during the Easter Mass, we do not know from explicit statements why the performance of plays was considered appropriate to these occasions. Similarly, about the elements of production—costumes, movements, gestures, stage-building, crowd control—we know very little in the case of other plays, except what can be inferred from chance observations. What Philippe tells us about his play is thus doubly valuable. We can conclude that his statements would apply in some degree to other plays of his time. And we can see how production details were integrated into the whole motive and conception of a play itself.

It is important to note, therefore, the importance to an understanding of this play which can be attributed to the method of biblical exegesis. The symbolic "action" of the play is the purging of the old law of sin and its replacement by the new law of grace embodied in Mary who is, by this replacement, made bride and queen in the renewed world. According to biblical exegetes, this action is the central fact of cosmic history and the conceptual framework for the understanding of the acts and signs in Scripture. This play has embodied and alluded to these symbols in rhetorical and liturgical forms suited to the full elucidation of their meaning. According to Philippe, the spectators will be fed with various doctrines, catholic fundamentals, which they will take in as symbolic details of the play itself. And, according to Philippe, the whole people will be so fully involved in the play, office, and sermon that on the one hand great effort will be required to keep them from mingling with (and even jostling) the performers, and that on the other hand the spirit of the play can be continued in processions and meals for the rest of the day. All of his attention to details of production is thus a manifestation of Philippe's profound sense of the relationship between mimetic actions and symbolic values.

This book has been arranged so as to emphasize this relationship, and thus to contribute to the understanding of fourteenth-century aesthetics. The introduction by Sister M. Catherine Rupp shows how the play is a unified reworking of the forms and symbols found in Scripture and the liturgy. The translation of the play itself is accompanied, as in the original manuscript, by Philippe's letter concerning the establishment of the feast of the Presentation and a note on the 1385 performance of the play at Avignon. The play is further supplemented by the retelling of Mary's early life, including her Presentation, to be found in Philippe's *Book of the Sacrament of Marriage*, since this version of the story also exemplifies, in a slightly different form, the allegorical imagination which underlies the play. All of these translations are followed by the Latin or French texts so that readers may with the aid of the translations appreciate the stylistic integrity of the originals and recognize the terms in Latin and French which their English equivalents do not fully translate. Taken as a whole, the book should make clear the extent to which Philippe de Mézières himself has the style and imagination of an important literary figure. It should also suggest that, even allowing for the prominence and learning of Philippe and his audience, other plays and other works of the fourteenth century must have been written in the same tradition of allegorical and exegetical symbolism.

ROBERT S. HALLER

University of Nebraska

Introduction

I. The Dramatist

Philippe de Mézières (1327–1405), the author of the Presentation Play, was a distinguished French soldier, diplomat, crusader, and writer of the fourteenth century.[1] His eventful military and diplomatic career, during which he was to plead with popes and counsel kings, led him over most of Europe, the Near East, and the principal Mediterranean lands. His association with the East was one of the major factors in his composition and promotion of the Presentation Play, and his life has been called one of the important links "that binds together the Orient and the Occident of the Middle Ages."[2]

Although Philippe's writings were varied in style and content, the corpus of his work reflects the almost consuming passion of his life—the Crusades. Born of a noble family in Picardy in 1327, he was initiated into arms in his youth, and gained considerable military experience in the Crusades before departing for Jerusalem about 1347. He was knighted after the Battle of Smyrna, but the sensitive crusader upon whom this honor was bestowed was disillusioned by the undisciplined conduct of his fellow military men. Out of his indignation

[1] The standard full-length biography is by N. Jorga, *Philippe de Mézières* (Bibliothèque de l'École des Hautes Études, no. 109; Paris, 1896). Jorga discusses at some length the problem of the dating of Philippe's birth. Since no definite date is given in records, a number of different dates, one as early as 1312, have been proposed. Jorga, however, cites 1327 as the year of his birth; and a more recent writer, G. W. Coopland (ed., *Le Songe du Vieil Pèlerin* [Cambridge: Cambridge University Press, 1969], p. 3), gives the birth date as 1327 without question. In general, I have used Jorga as my authority for biographical data, although he admits that some lacunae exist concerning certain periods of Philippe's life.

[2] Sister Mary Jerome Kishpaugh, O.P., *The Feast of the Presentation of the Virgin Mary in the Temple: An Historical and Literary Study* (Washington: Catholic University Press, 1941), p. 92.

over their unscrupulous behavior grew his plans for a new order of chivalry, *Novo religio Passionis*, plans which he began to formulate in 1367 or 1368 and which materialized in redactions in 1384 and 1396. His projected rule for a new order of the Knights of the Passion was an idealized one, grounded solidly in the spiritual values of prayer and sacrifice. It is not surprising that most of the combatants, unaccustomed to discipline and restraint either by authority or by self-control, and interested only in the personal gains which the Crusades had to offer rather than in the nobility of the cause, would refuse to embrace the spiritual and austere way of life which Philippe's strict and rigid order had to offer.

In 1347 Philippe, returning from a trip to Jerusalem, visited the court of Hugh IV, King of Cyprus, and formed a friendship with Peter of Lusignan, then Count of Tripoli. At the king's death in 1358, Peter ascended the throne and shortly thereafter requested that Philippe return to the island to become its chancellor, an invitation which he accepted. Here Philippe became the intimate friend of Peter Thomas, the papal legate and a saintly prelate, who later, in 1364, was appointed patriarch of Constantinople. He therefore had the support of two powerful personalities, one a temporal ruler and the other a spiritual leader, whose interests and activities complemented his own.

During the next few years all three—king, chancellor, and papal legate—worked tirelessly promoting an offensive campaign against the infidels. They traveled extensively throughout Europe endeavoring to stir up enthusiasm for the Crusades, soliciting men and money, negotiations which often involved delicate diplomatic problems between the papal palace and the royal courts. In 1365, when conditions looked favorable for an attack on the Saracens, they left Europe to return to Cyprus to make immediate preparations, but great disappointments were in store for them when promises of desperately needed supplies were not fulfilled. Peter I was forced to begin the Crusade of 1365 with such volunteers as he could collect at random. Under these adverse conditions, the capture and the occupation of Alexandria in October, 1365, fleeting victory that it was, caused great amazement and jubilation. Hope for success was restored and Philippe returned to Cyprus and continued crusading plans with renewed ardor, though a few months later, in January, 1366, he suffered a terrible loss in the death of his beloved friend, Peter Thomas, whom he affectionately called "Father."

In June, 1366, Philippe was delegated to Venice, to Avignon, and to the sovereigns of western Europe to obtain help for Cyprus against Egypt, but his efforts were in vain. Political and economic factors influenced European leaders to such an extent that even Pope Urban V advised peace with the sultan. Disappointed and heartbroken, Philippe returned to Avignon and remained there for some time (1367–1368) writing the biography of Peter Thomas,[3] seeking recruits for his projected chivalric order, and drawing up his *Prefacio* and *Epistola* for the regulation of it. He returned to Cyprus in 1368 but was in Venice in 1369 when word reached him that Peter I had been assassinated by some of his subjects who had either suffered under his heavy ruling hand or had felt contempt for the degradation of his personal life. His death was a fatal blow to Philippe's crusading endeavors, for as a practical man-of-affairs he well knew that without the active support of a temporal ruler, the death knell would be tolling for the project which was his life's greatest ambition. Followers and friends of Peter I were being persecuted and put to death so Philippe dared not return to Cyprus, which in his agony he called *Haceldama* or Field of Blood. The new king of Cyprus, Peter II, however, continued good relations with Philippe by correspondence and in 1370 appointed him his representative at the coronation of Pope Gregory the Eleventh at the Papal Court, then situated at Avignon.

Through Philippe's efforts, the feast of the Presentation of the Blessed Virgin Mary was celebrated with full papal approval on November 21, 1372, at the Church of the Friars Minor in Avignon. In Cyprus Philippe had been impressed by the devout celebration of the feast and had determined to introduce the rite to the Western Church, where it was little known. His enthusiasm for a feast in Mary's honor is not surprising, for his devotion to the Blessed Virgin was lifelong. As an infant he had been baptized in Amiens in the beautiful cathedral of Notre-Dame, a great Gothic edifice dedicated to the Virgin, and had later pursued his studies with considerable seriousness at the cathedral school. In his youth he had taken Mary for his patronness and vowed to have a special devotion to her during his entire life; this veneration and confidence in her as an advocate

---

[3] *Vita S Petri Thomasii* (Antwerp, 1659). This book is invaluable for historical information on the Alexandrian expedition. The vivid description of high hopes and bitter disillusionment rank it high among the Latin literature of the period.

appears in all his writings.[4] In a letter he indicates that he was instrumental in having the feast celebrated at Venice several years before 1372 where it was accompanied by a dramatic representation.[5] Encouraged by the reception of the feast in Italy, Philippe began to seek papal approval for it; in his letter he says that he "presented the whole office to [Pope Gregory] humbly, along with the musical notations," asking that it "might be ordered to be celebrated everywhere in the lands of the apostolic authority, or at least be allowed to be celebrated at the will of the devotees." Pope Gregory the Eleventh, himself a devout follower of the Virgin Mary, consulted a body of cardinals before granting permission for (rather than ordering) the celebration of the feast by the faithful. Although no specific evidence exists as proof that the 1372 celebration of the feast at Avignon included the Presentation Play, a note concerning a dramatic performance at Avignon in 1385 contains a brief description of the play which corresponds in general, if not in details, to the representation in the manuscript which must have had ecclesiastical approval.[6] Through Philippe's enthusiasm and zeal the feast soon extended to many sections of Europe.

In 1373 Philippe's diplomatic talents were again utilized when Charles V, a friend of long standing who shared his hopes for the deliverance of Jerusalem, appointed him a royal counsellor of the French court and the tutor of the future Charles VI; he also honored

[4] Jorga, *Philippe de Mézières*, p. 29.

[5] See below, p. 53. There is no other known reference to this early celebration at Venice, but Jorga deduces from Philippe's sojourns in that city that the date would be between 1365 and 1372, with 1370 being a likely date (*Philippe de Mézières*, pp. 236–244, 402–404). It seems from the letter that there was more than one celebration in Italy.

[6] See below, pp. 51–58, 67–70, for complete translations of the Letter and Note. Grace Frank, *The Medieval French Drama* (Oxford: Clarendon Press, 1954), p. 64, expresses the possibility of a dramatic performance in 1372: "Philippe de Mézières, for example, brought to Avignon, perhaps in 1372, surely in 1385, a dramatic performance of the *Presentation of the Virgin Mary in the Temple* that contains every element necessary for a supremely moving spectacle." Karl Young, *The Drama of the Medieval Church* (Oxford: The Clarendon Press, 1933), 2:227, records a similar belief: "Although Philippe de Mézières does not mention the matter specifically, we naturally infer that this celebration on November 21st, 1372, included the *repraesentatio figurato* which had previously been performed at Venice. In any case, we have a record of a dramatic performance, before Mass on the feast of the Presentation, at Avignon in 1385."

Philippe with a pension. Philippe's enthusiasm for a wider celebration of the feast of the Presentation soon involved Charles V, who promoted this apostolate by celebrating the festival in the royal chapel on November 21, 1373, with a large assembly of prelates and nobles, and wrote letters in 1374 with pleas for the adoption of the feast.[7]

In 1380 Charles V died; Philippe, saddened by the death of his friend and master and by the confused political state effected by the inexperience and temperament of Charles VI, retired to the religious house conducted by the Celestines in Paris, where he imitated the life of the religious but remained a member of the laity. In this peaceful and prayerful atmosphere he was to spend the remaining twenty-five years of his life, writing and enjoying close contacts with old friends, many of whom were important personages of his time.[8]

Like his fourteenth-century contemporaries, Dante and Chaucer, Philippe was disturbed by irregularities of political and ecclesiastical powers, and in a vast work written in French prose and completed in 1389, *Le Songe du vieil pèlerin*, he skilfully used the allegorical cadre to discuss corruptions of both tiara and crown. The "Old Pilgrim" is Philippe himself, usually called "Ardent Desire" in the text, who takes a journey throughout the known world in quest of peoples and nations where Christianity is faithfully preached and observed, and through his travels demonstrates the desperate plight of Christendom at that time. In his penchant for the allegorical, Philippe commonly selected biblical characters and events, as in his epistle to Richard II, where Charles VI and Richard II become Moses and Aaron.[9] In *Le Songe* his allegory depicts the spiritual ascent on Mount Sinai of the New Moses, Charles VI, who after a prolonged novitiate under the allegorical Queen Truth, finally receives the emblem of royalty, not by hereditary birth, but by moral superiority. The learning and experience which Philippe had accumulated in half a century of service in the East and in the West in his relationships with popes,

---

[7] Jorga, *Philippe de Mézières*, pp. 422–423, states that Charles V wrote several letters urging the extension of the feast: one to the dean of Sainte-Marie de Melun, another to the masters and students of the College of Champayne at Paris, and a third to Nicolas d'Arcis, Bishop of Auxerre.

[8] Ibid., p. 447. Some of the personages Jorga mentions as being close friends of Philippe are Bureau de la Rivière, Hugues and Pierre d'Ailly, and Pierre de Luxembourg.

[9] This letter, "Epistre au Roi Richart," is in MS B.M. Royal B.vi. See *Les oeuvres de Jean Froissart*, ed. Kervyn de Lettenhove (1867–1876), 15:200, 388–391.

kings, princes, and men of all classes in medieval society is reflected in his remarkable insight into the significant events of the times, particularly the Great Schism and the Hundred Years' War. Dora Bell, who has made a study of the work, asserts that this great allegory "deserves a place as a forerunner of the masterpieces of medieval literature not only for the importance of the matter but also for its literary qualities." [10]

In his later years Philippe devoted himself to writing a symbolic treatise on marriage, *Le Livre du Sacrament de Mariage et du reconfort des dames mariées*. Both the method and the content of this work are typical of Philippe's lifetime literary efforts: he uses the allegorical method, comparing the marriages he describes to the union of a fine diamond with a fine ruby; and the Virgin Mary plays a prominent role, for she is the "fine ruby" representing the Church. [11]

Philippe de Mézières was a great and influential figure of the fourteenth century, not only in France, but in the world at large. During his long life—he died at the age of seventy-eight on May 29, 1405—he played a part, a principal one, in most of the great events of the century. He combined the characteristics of a man of action with a contemplative spirit, and those of the practical politician and soldier with idealistic theories of statecraft and chivalry. Yet he was single-minded in purpose, and he firmly believed that the restoration of order in the world was dependent on every man's commitment to moral values. Fortunately, his noble spirit and his largesse of ideas were combined with the gift of a literary style that ranks him high among the writers of his period. [12] Though it would indeed be presumptuous to contend that Philippe will ever attain the literary stature of Dante or Chaucer, one may safely state that he is gradually growing in prominence and that in the future he will assume his rightful position among medieval writers.

II. The Play

Philippe de Mézières' Presentation Play is difficult to classify in a particular dramatic category. It is usually referred to as a

[10] Bell, *Études sur le Songe du vieil pèlerin* (Geneva: E. Drox, 1955), p. 9. G. W. Coopland (cited above, n. 1), has recently edited *Le Songe*.

[11] See below, pp. 75–81, for the translation of the second section of this work.

[12] See Jorga, *Philippe de Mézières*, p. 511.

Latin liturgical drama. Such drama was written in Latin, acted by clerics, and performed in a church as an expansion and integral part of the liturgy. The Presentation Play differs from these criteria in that, though it is written in Latin, Philippe indicates that it may be presented in the vernacular; in that the actors are not required to be clergy, although the bishop does play a major role and some of the other performers very well may have been clerics;[13] and in that it is ceremonial and preparatory to the Office and the Mass, and its structure is such that it could conceivably be performed independently of the liturgy. Philippe's production also differs from the lavish vernacular mystery cycles which were performed on street platforms or pageant wagons during this period of the late Middle Ages, even though he does intend for the procession and festivities to continue after the performance in church.

The Presentation Play is important from various points of view: to the liturgical historian, because it provides insights into the sophistication of a drama associated with the liturgy; to the literary historian, because the author is known when medieval drama is usually anonymous; to the historian of the theater, because it contains profuse stage directions at a time when this was not the custom; and to the literary critic, because of the explicitness of the aesthetics of the play.

Fortunately Philippe was a careful archivist and assiduously preserved his manuscripts in a book which passed from the Celestine monastery in Paris, in which he was residing as a layman at the time

---

[13] Young, *Drama of the Medieval Church*, has provided a valuable sourcebook in editing many tropes and plays of this period. O. B. Hardison, Jr., in his recent book, *Christian Rite and Christian Drama in the Middle Ages* (Baltimore: Johns Hopkins Press, 1965) though disagreeing with Young on what constitutes the essence of drama, supports the theory that the Church in her age-old liturgy recreated and fostered the dramatic idea. George La Piana, in "The Byzantine Iconography of the Presentation of the Virgin Mary to the Temple and a Latin Religious Pageant," in *Late Classical and Mediaeval Studies in Honor of Albert Mathias Friend, Jr.*, ed. Kurt Weitzmann (Princeton: Princeton University Press, 1955), p. 267, states: "In our *Representatio*, on the contrary, the performers are 'actors,' dressed in special costumes according to their role in the play. Their speeches, though taken from sacred texts, have no liturgical character. On the other hand, neither is the *Representatio* an independent play, because it is inserted into the liturgical celebration and is a part of it, especially its last scene which takes place at the altar with the bishop in pontifical robes speaking as the Voice of God. Instead of a drama, the *Representatio* may be called more properly a religious pageant connected with a liturgical office."

of his death, to the Bibliothèque Nationale, where it was discovered by Professor Marius Sepet in the late nineteenth century. At that time Sepet announced that the manuscript was "a document most precious for the history of the *mise-en-scène*."[14] At the death of his confrere, Anatole Lefoullon, who had intended to publish the document, Sepet suggested to his friend, Karl Young, that he do the editing. Professor Young accepted the recommendation, and in 1911 published the two most important articles of the manuscript, the drama and the letter referring to it, and also the note about the 1385 production. In 1933 he re-edited the complete text of the play in the second volume of his *Drama of the Medieval Church*, devoting several pages to a summary of the play but making no critical evaluation of it except to remark that it is a "true play," for "the story is completely presented in the form of action, and the characters concerned in it are elaborately impersonated."[15]

Although the play has been widely admired by critics for the past sixty years, little has been done in the way of critical analysis. In 1941 Sister Mary Jerome Kishpaugh devoted a chapter to Philippe de Mézières in *The Feast of the Presentation of the Virgin Mary in the Temple: An Historical and Literary Study*, but since her study is concerned with the origin and history of this liturgical festival, she traces its spread in the West through Philippe's pious zeal and concerns herself with facts rather than with interpretation.[16] The first critical study of the play was undertaken by the present author in 1967, at which time the meaning of the play was explicated using the method of medieval exegetes.[17]

In both his Letter and in the introduction to the dramatic representation, Philippe alludes to the symbolic value of the acts depicted in the play. In the letter, after discussing the five-fold variety of spiritual food offered by the feast, he declares that all the mysteries and fundamentals of our human redemption are foreshadowed in the Presentation of the Virgin. In the first paragraph of the Presentation Play, he enunciates a principle prevalent during the Middle Ages: the mind can be stimulated to recognize the invisible and visible mysteries of

---

[14] Sepet, *Les Prophètes du Christ* (Paris, 1878), p. 45, n. 1.

[15] Young, *Drama of the Medieval Church*, 2:244. The first editing is in *PMLA* 26 (1911):181–234.

[16] She traces the history of the festival from the accounts in the apocryphal gospels, and its growth through the Eastern and Western Church until it reached an accepted place in the calendar of the Universal Church.

[17] M. Catherine Rupp. O.S.M., "Medieval Dramatic Meaning and Philippe de Mézières," (Ph.D. diss., University of Nebraska, 1967).

God through visible things, signs, and works—a process of understanding which, as he says, is in accord with apostolic teaching. And the language of the play is liturgical, taken primarily from Scripture and from the writings of the Fathers of the Church. Hence the use of medieval exegetical principles is not only valid but necessary if one is to discover the true meaning of the play.

Most medieval writers define allegory simply as saying one thing while meaning another, but the system is a very complex one. While medieval allegory represents a continuation of a technique which extends from the sixth century B.C. until the eighteenth century, during which course of time the tradition underwent many changes, adapting itself to many stylistic and cultural modifications, this discussion shall be limited to one aspect of the medieval theory of allegory, namely, that which designates levels of meaning in the Bible, a theory built on the foundation of the principles enunciated in St. Paul's Epistles and St. Augustine's *De Doctrina Christiani*. St. Paul's view held that the teachings of Christ make it possible to see the spirit beneath the surface of the Old Testament, or the glory beneath the "veil."[18] On the basis of St. Paul's theory, systems of interpretation were gradually elaborated, especially by St. Augustine whose principle, "Scripture . . . does not prescribe except charity, nor blame except cupidity,"[19] became the guide-line for medieval exegetes. Once the veil had been removed and it was possible to see beneath the literal or visible surface of signs the invisible things of God, then these would have implications for the Church (allegory), for the spiritual life of the individual (tropology), and for the afterlife (anagogy). The literal or historical sense was held in reverence as the foundation of the higher spiritual sense. Terminology for the different levels of meaning varied with different exegetes, but the fundamental idea is the same: the nucleus of the spirit is derived from the cortex of the letter.[20]

[18] 2 Corinthians 3:13–16.

[19] "Non autem praecipit Scripture nisi charitatem, ned culpat nisi cupiditatem" (*De Doctrina Christiani*, 3.15.10, in *Patrologiae Cursus Completus Series Latinae*, ed. J. P. Migne [Paris, 1844–1864], 34:71). Henceforth the Latin Series of the *Patrologia* will be designated as *P.L.*, and the Greek Series as *P.G.*

[20] Some studies useful in illuminating this tradition are: Edgar de Bruyne, *Études d'esthetique medievale* (Bruges: De Tempel, 1946); Henri de Lubac, S.J., *Exegese Médiévale: Les Quatre Sens de l'Ecriture* (Paris: Aubier, 1959), 3 vols.; and D. W. Robertson, Jr., "Some Principles of Medieval

The great exegetes would have been familiar to any man learned in Scripture. Origen (184–253), Ambrose (339–397), Cassiodorus (490–583), Rabanus Maurus (776–856), Alanus de Insulis (1114–1202), Rupert of Deutz (1075–1129), and Honorius of Autun (1080–1156) were among those who recognized the literal and historical sense of Scripture but preferred allegorical and moral interpretations in their commentaries. A study of the works of Guillaume Durand (ca. 1230–1298), Bishop of Mende, is especially helpful in revealing the symbolical value the medieval audience attached to the total liturgical nexus which serves as the setting for the play.

With medieval exegesis serving as a method of interpretation, we shall direct our attention to the form and content of the play itself. The dramatic form of the Presentation Play takes the lineal shape of a procession of the participants and clergy; the *Laudes Mariae*, a series of praises chanted by nine white-robed angels; the dramatic encounters between Anna and Joachim, between Michael and Lucifer, and between the allegorical figures of Ecclesia and Synagoga; and lastly, the *figuratio*, the dramatic action which imitates the child Mary being presented in the temple. Hopefully, through observation of the major themes in the various parts, the play will emerge as more unified than may first be apparent.

The Procession

Philippe gives precise directions for the procession of the characters and the clergy as they enter the church. After the participants are vested and costumed in the chapter house, the clergy lead the procession, followed by nine angels, Synagoga, Ecclesia, two young musicians, two young virgins, Mary with Gabriel and Raphael, Joachim and Anna, Michael and Lucifer, and lastly, a group of approved laymen. Philippe carefully describes what each member of the cast is to wear and what emblem he is to carry. Mary's costume is to be white and gold, symbolizing her purity and virginity, and the radiance of her charity. One of the two small virgins who accom-

Aesthetics," in *A Preface to Chaucer: Studies in Medieval Perspectives* (Princeton: Princeton University Press, 1962). See also Barry Caplan's "The Four Senses of Scriptural Interpretation and the Medieval Theory of Preaching," *Speculum* 4 (1929):282–290, and Edward A. Bloom's "The Allegorical Principle," *ELH* 16 (1951):163–190.

pany her is to be dressed in green, symbolizing the humility of Mary, and the other in blue, symbolizing the faith and hope of Mary. The nine angels, representing the nine choirs of angels, are to wear white vestments, wings, and birettas, and are to be divided into three orders, the first order having their birettas embroidered in red, the second order in blue, and the third order in white. Ecclesia is to be dressed in gold and wear a golden crown with lilies and precious stones; fastened to her breast is to be a silver chalice symbolizing the New Testament. Synagoga is to be dressed in a drab color with a dark cloth covering her head and a black cloth over her eyes. Joachim is to be dressed in an alb, a stole, and a *pluvialis;* he is to have a cloth draped about his head and neck. Anna is to be dressed entirely in white linen. Michael is to be dressed handsomely in armor, with his helmet having a gilt crown symbolizing a victorious soldier and Christ triumphant, while Lucifer is to look ugly with horns, fangs, and a horrible face.

Characters in the procession are to carry the following emblems: the nine angels are to carry lilies; Synagoga a red banner with the insignia of Rome in her left hand and two stone tablets in her right; Ecclesia a long gilded cross in her left hand and a gilt sphere symbolizing the universal dominion of the Church in her right; the two maidens lighted candles; Mary a lighted candle and a dove; Joachim a glass full of red wine; Anna a round loaf of white bread; Michael a flashing sword in his right hand and an iron chain in his left; and Lucifer a hook in his right hand or an iron hook over his shoulder and holding Michael's chain in his left hand. Philippe explains only some of the symbolism of clothing and emblems; he apparently assumes that his medieval audience would understand much of it without its significance being stated.

The bishop or archbishop who is to celebrate the Mass begins singing the *Salve Regina,* a hymn which salutes Mary as Queen. Mary is being praised as the one who is to fulfill the prophecies by virtue of her divine maternity and ultimately to reign as Queen of Heaven, but since she is a figure for the Church, the hymn is also an encomium for the Church.[21] When the clergy finish the *Salve Regina,* an angel begins a rondel in the vernacular in honor of the

[21] St. Ambrose was one of the first to teach that Mary is a figure of the Church (*Expositio Evangelii Secundum Lucam,* bk. 2, *P.L.,* 11:1555). See also Honorius of Autun, *Sigillum Beatae Marie Ubi Exponuntur Cantica Canticorum, P.L.,* 172:499.

Virgin, and the other angels, together with Ecclesia, Gabriel, Raphael, and the musicians respond; then all are silent except the angels, who continue the antiphonal singing until the procession reaches the stage built in the middle of the church.

During the Middle Ages the procession to the altar was considered to be figurative, as Durand proposes: "The procession itself is the way which leads to the celestial homeland."[22] Such processions were an integral part of the celebration of the great feasts of the liturgical year; Durand specifically mentions the procession in conjunction with the Feast of the Purification, and the mystical meaning he attributes to it there is relevant to the significance of the procession for this Marian feast. Durand states that the general procession denotes that which the Blessed Mary and Joseph made to the temple; and that those in the procession who chant before the balustrade symbolize the prophets announcing the Nativity of the Lord and his mercy, while those who respond do so in the joy of those who received this mercy from the Lord.[23] Again, he notes that the two alternating choirs are the Jews and the Gentiles who precede Christ and chant his praises.[24] Durand sees in the six orders of clergy who precede the pontiff or bishop the predecessors of Christ from the beginning of the Old Law—patriarchs, prophets, kings, princes, shepherds, and wise men. It becomes apparent, then, that the medieval mystical meaning of a procession moving toward the "celestial homeland" is related to the Old Law–New Law theme which looks upon the Old Law as prefiguring the New Law, and the New Law as fulfilling the Old Law, with Christ at the pivotal point between the two.

In both Durand's and Philippe's procession the essential consideration is not order of precedence as to hierarchic rule, the normal usage for the processional marshal, but order as determined by symbolic temporal considerations. Both are similar to Dante's processional where the Book of the Old Law precedes the emblems of the Church and Christ, who are in turn followed by the Book of the

---

[22] Guillaume Durand, *Rational où Manuel Des Divins Offices*, tr. into French by Charles Barthelemy (Paris, 1854), vol. 2, bk. 4, p. 52. (All translations from Durand into English are my own. I have used the French form of his name throughout rather than the Latin, "Gulielmus Durandi"; he is also known as Durandus, Durantis, or Duranti.)

[23] Ibid., vol. 5, bk. 7, p. 42.

[24] Ibid., vol. 2, bk. 4, p. 52.

New Law.[25] Philippe's processional, however, differs from Dante's and Durand's in that Mary, with the two virgins, is the pivotal point rather than Christ; with them she represents faith, hope, and charity, the theological virtues of the New Law. His procession also differs in that the symbolic temporal order is not so rigidly observed: though Mary is preceded by the clergy, the angels (the alternating choirs), and Synagoga, symbols of the Old Law, she is also preceded by Ecclesia, a symbol of the New Law, and is followed by Joachim and Anna, who carry emblems—the bread and wine—which suggest that they represent the last of the Old Law and the first of the New.[26] The general order, nonetheless, is a symbolic temporal order which extends from the beginning to the end of time: the angels existed from before the world, and Michael, with the captive Lucifer, as in the Book of Revelation, suggests the end of time.

The Laudes Mariae

After the colorful procession of characters has wended its way into the church, Gabriel ascends the first stage and silences the crowd. Then Mary, with a joyful countenance, ascends the stairs alone, holding either the dove and the candle, or carrying the dove with both hands while Raphael holds her candle. Philippe does not specifically mention fifteen steps in this production, but the Note about the 1385 performance does; and in his Letter Philippe speaks of "Mary's mature ascent of the fifteen steps," relating them to the fifteen Gradual Psalms.[27] These Psalms (120–134) constituted the Pilgrim Psalter, a popular devotion with which a complex mystical interpretation was associated. During the Middle Ages it was thought to have been chanted in the temple on the fifteen steps from the

[25] See *Purgatorio*, 29–30. Dante's symbolic procession begins with seven candlesticks, which represent the gifts of the Holy Spirit, followed by elders dressed in white, the color of faith, who represent the books of the Old Testament. The four Gospel creatures are dressed in green, the color of hope, and surround the chariot of the Church Triumphant drawn by a griffon representing Christ in his divine and human natures. Three nymphs at the right represent faith, hope, and love, while the four figures to the left represent the four cardinal virtues prudence, temperance, fortitude, and justice. The final figures in the procession, all crowned with red to represent the charity of the New Testament, represent the Epistles and the Apocalypse.

[26] For a fuller discussion of their emblems, see below, p. xxxiii.

[27] See below, p. 57.

court of the women to the court of Israel. The ascent of the steps was taken to be an allegorical journey whereby man moved from virtue to virtue in the ladder of perfection, as Durand and others testify:

> . . . the prophets continually show us, in the fifteen psalms, the degrees which a holy man has erected in his heart. Jacob saw this ladder of which the highest part touched the sky. By these degrees are meant, in a manner suitable and clear, the degrees of virtues by which one mounts to the altar, that is to say, to Christ, according to this word of the Psalmist: "And they shall march and shall elevate themselves from virtue to virtue." [28]

In the only other extant medieval play on the Presentation of the Virgin, *Mary in the Temple,* one of the five Marian plays of the Hegge Cycle of the English mystery plays, which probably dates several decades later than Philippe's drama, the bishop explicitly mentions the fifteen degrees and the fifteen psalms:

> Thou xalt be the dawtere of God eternalle
> If the fyftene grees thou may ascende . . .
> The fyftene psalmys in memorye of this mayde say, Maria! [29]

In Philippe's play Mary ascends the steps silently; in the English mystery play her ascent is marked by the recitation of a quatrain from the fifteen gradual psalms on each step or "degree," during which the child Mary reflects on such virtues as confidence in God, hope in immortality, contempt of vain glory, faith, and brotherly concord. When she reaches the altar she falls on her knees and makes seven petitions to God for help in serving and loving him faithfully. Philippe's Mary is not articulate, but the mystical meanings are nevertheless implied.

When all the participants have taken their assigned places— Joachim and Anna to the right and left of Mary, the two virgins at Mary's feet, Synagoga and Ecclesia on stools to the east and west of Mary—each of the nine white-robed angels in turn bows reverently before the child Mary and recites short lyrical passages, the *Laudes Mariae,* in praise of the Virgin's special place in the plan of redemption.

[28] Durand, *Rational,* vol. 1, bk. 1, p. 40.
[29] "Mary in the Temple," in *Ludus Coventriae,* ed. K. S. Block (London: Oxford University Press, 1922), p. 74.

In tracing the generic tradition of the *laudes*, especially as it evolved in the Middle Ages and was used by Philippe, it appears that the Canticles and Psalms of the Old Testament provide the archetypal pattern.[30] This highly stylized conventional form of address begins almost every line with the anaphoric use of "Hail," "Bless," or "Praise," followed by synonyms or laudatory metaphors extolling the qualities and characteristics of the person being eulogized. Most of the verses which the angels recite are biblical passages applied to Mary and taken from the large storehouse of *Laudes Virginis* in both Greek and Latin patristic and liturgical literature.[31] Another possible influence on Philippe's choice of this genre may have been the *laudes regiae*, a series of liturgical acclamations and reverential hails to popes and kings sung at medieval coronations and festival days. Since Mary is addressed as Queen in the verses of the angels, Philippe may have adapted the literary form of the *laudes* to emphasize her claim to royalty. The tradition of using angelic song to localize heaven was quite generally adopted in medieval drama, and in Philippe's play the angels singing the *laudes* do create the locus of heaven, placing this part of the drama outside of time. This supports the medieval attitude toward Mary, namely, that because of her special attributes, especially her humility, virginity, and divine motherhood, virtues lauded by Philippe's angels, Mary is honored as the Queen of Heaven, a Queen who can help weary pilgrims along life's way to reach the heavenly Jerusalem.

Understanding the meaning of the figurative language in the *laudes* depends on the hearer's ability to perceive allegorical and typological significance beneath the letter of the Old Testament images. Much of the figurative language is taken from the Old Testament Canticle of Canticles. This Song of Solomon is in fact the source of two of the most important passages in the entire play— the opening lines of the first angel in the *Laudes Mariae*, "Who is she who ascends from the desert as a wisp of smoke, from the fragrance of myrrh and frankincense?" and the final words of the dramatic presentation in which the bishop invites Mary to ascend the altar steps: "Come my Beloved, come my Dove, because there is no spot

---

[30] Among the psalms which could be classified in the generic form of the *laudes* are: 103, 104, 105, 106, 110, 112, 116, 133, 134, 135, 137, 143, 144, 145, 146, 147, 148, 149, and 150. Psalm 103 uses anaphoric language closely analogous to the *Laudes Mariae*.

[31] George La Piana, "Byzantine Iconography," p. 266.

on you. Come from Lebanon, my Chosen from eternity, that I might accept you as Bride for my beloved Son." Obviously Philippe must have attached a special significance to these passages or he would not have placed them in the key positions at the beginning and the end of the play.

In order to ascertain the meaning Philippe had in mind in using the language of the Canticle, one must look for commonly accepted medieval interpretations of the book. The Canticle of Canticles was from very early times interpreted allegorically; Jewish exegesis considered it a representation of Yahweh's dealings with Israel from the Exodus to the return from exile, citing the writings of the prophets who frequently represent the relations between Yahweh and Israel as that of husband and wife.[32] The early Fathers of the Church applied the allegory to the union which exists between Christ and his Church in the New Testament, citing passages in the Gospels which describe Christ as the Bridegroom, and the foundation of the Church as a marriage feast.[33]

Origen (185–284) was not the first Christian writer to compose a commentary on the Canticle, but his is the first great work of Christian mysticism and the fountainhead for all future allegorical writers on the Canticle; in delineating the Bride as the Church, he set a precedent that was to be followed by writers and preachers for centuries to come. His exegesis indicates that the Fathers of the Church were groping for a figurative story which might represent the Church in love with God; at that time no *De Ecclesia* treatise existed, and this book from the Old Testament offered rich and inviting material to portray a vital and warmly beloved Church. Origen extends his allegorical interpretation of the Bridegroom-Bride relationship to the union, first, between God and the Church, secondly, between Christ and his Church, and thirdly, between Christ and the faithful soul.[34]

The twelfth-century exegete, Honorius, in the prologue to his exposition on the Canticle, gives almost every conceivable marriage on all four levels of interpretation. On the allegorical level, he discusses

[32] See Ezechiel 16:3–4, Isaias 54:6–17, Jeremias 2:2–3, and Osee 2:19–23. Israel is portrayed as adulteress in Isaias 50:1, Jeremias 3:1–14, Ezechiel 16:1–58, and Osee 2:1–13.

[33] Matthew 9:15, John 3:29, 2 Corinthians 11:2, Ephesians 5:23–32, Acts of the Apostles 30:9 and Matthew 22:14.

[34] Origen, *Homilias in Canticum Canticorum*, P.G., 13:37–217.

the mystical marriages which represent the way in which the Word of God joined itself to flesh and became man, and the way in which Christ joined God and man in the universal Church by associating himself with the faithful through the uniting of his own body with them. On the tropological level, Honorius sees in the Song the marriages of the mind joined to Christ through love, and of the mind joined to the Holy Spirit, from which union the offspring of good works are born. He also sees anagogical marriages, those which stand for the union, after judgment, when the entire Church will be transferred to the heavenly Jerusalem and enjoy the vision of the God-head in the glory of his "bridal chamber."[35]

Although the tradition dating from Origen and the Church Fathers which determines the Bride as Ecclesia, or the soul, or both, was rich and profuse, by the time of Philippe's play the Bride was frequently interpreted as Mary; the Canticle had already been incorporated into the liturgy of the Church for the feast of the Assumption of the Blessed Virgin and, in some churches, for the feast of the Nativity.[36] Mary was frequently equated with the Church, as the first soul of the Church. It is of course the tradition of Mary as the Bride of the Canticle that Philippe primarily adopts, though the equation of Mary with the Church is also implied, particularly in the speech of Ecclesia later.[37]

Besides the bridal concept in the language from the Canticle, the bridal imagery is made still more explicit by the words of the fourth angel who acclaims Mary as "she who will be made the Bride . . . of God," and the eighth angel who exclaims, "O admirable bride!" The idea of a mystical marriage is conveyed not only by the use of figurative language but it is also brought out visually by Mary's costume. Philippe directs that she be dressed in a long white gown with a white mantle in the manner of a bride; his choice of white for Mary's costume is in contrast to the traditional medieval choice of blue and red. Appropriately, since Mary vowed virginity in the temple, both the attire and the phrases from the Canticle in the Presentation Play are closely related to the dress and wording of the ceremony whereby medieval virgins, "Brides of Christ," vowed their love to God. The color white was a commonly accepted symbol for purity and innocence; in addition, Durand sees an important

[35] Honorius of Autun, *Expositio in Cantica Canticorum*, *P.L.*, 162:349.
[36] Durand, *Rational*, vol. 5, bk. 7, p. 78.
[37] See below, p. xxxiv.

tropological meaning in the virgins' divesting themselves of their old attire and investing themselves in the new white robes, namely, that they are putting off the "old man" and putting on the "new," a well-known admonition of St. Paul (Ephesians 4:21–24). Philippe specifies that Mary's head is to be uncovered; Durand describes the consecrated virgins unveiled and he gives the following symbolic reasons, something Philippe omits:

> They come bare-headed to meet the prelate . . . . Now they represent that which we read in the Canticle; "Raise me, my beloved, my betrothed; show me your face, and let your voice sound in my ears." The bare head denotes also in a suitable manner the abandonment and the entire renunciation of the things of this world. They enter in the church bare-headed also in order to denote that, as beautiful and agreeable fiancées in the eyes of the Spouse, they are introduced into his house.[38]

Philippe's concern with mystical marriages is developed at greater length in *Le Livre du Sacrament de Marriage et du reconfort des dames mariées*. One section of this book describes the marriage of Christ and the Church at the Crucifixion and another section treats of the marriage of God and man in the Incarnation. In the latter, Philippe points out that God made Mary beautiful and holy "so as to be mother and bride of his blessed son, Jesus Christ."[39]

During the Middle Ages the concept of marriage assumed a wider extension of meaning, so that every soul who avoids sin is the spouse of Christ, for he thereby preserves the marriage contracted at baptism. Likewise, a man faithful to the marriage between the spirit and the flesh, or reason and sensuality, is a sharer in the divine marriage between Christ and the Church. Since in the apostolic tradition bishops and priests inherited the place of Christ in reference to the Church, a bishop was considered married to his diocese and the priest was regarded as the husband of his parish.

Many of the exegetes also analyze the other images in this passage from the Canticles in terms of ascent, movement, and journeying. These analyses may be considered applicable to the Presentation

---

[38] Durand, *Rational*, vol. 1, bk. 2, p. 190. In the same place he adds: "These robes must be appropriate and white, in order to signify that, as they are the fiancées to the Son of God, they must in future preserve themselves from all soil and preserve themselves in purity and holiness."

[39] See below, p. 75.

Play in that they are, in a sense, an extension of the implications of Mary's ascent up the temple stairs, and also because in his Letter Philippe says that the third food of the Feast of the Presentation is "the contemplation of the preparation of our redemption in Mary."[40] The exegete Honorius says the Church prepares for its final redemption by traveling through the desert, moving as a column of smoke when it weeps for its sins; it gives an aromatic odor of virtue when it is mortified for the sake of Christ; it offers incense to God when it lives a holy life and gives good example. The desert is the Gentile nations without the fertile fruits of virtue; the wisp is the fear of the Lord, through which the Church ascends to wisdom; the smoke is holy desire, created by the fire of divine love; the myrrh is the suffering of martyrs; the incense is the sacrifice of confessors; and all the powders of the perfumer is the devotion of the faithful to Christ.[41]

Rupert of Deutz describes the six images as six steps the soul must take, with the help of the Church, to ascend to perfection—steps very like those involved in the reception of the seven gifts of the Holy Spirit, which will be discussed later. The steps in his ladder mounting to perfection begin with fear, ascend to the smoke of compunction, move to the aroma of virtue, thence to the myrrh of mortification, on to the incense of confession, and finally mount to the powders of the perfumers, Christ-likeness.[42]

Immediately following the passage from the Canticle, the first angel delivers another biblical quotation commonly known as the Prophecy of Isaias:

> Is it not that staff which will arise from the root of Jesse, and will not a flower come forth from that root, and the spirit of the Lord rest on him, the spirit of wisdom and knowledge, the spirit of learning and counsel, the spirit of piety and courage, and the spirit of the fear of the Lord?

Alanus de Insulis speaks of both the root of Jesse and the Bride of the Canticle in the same passage, equating both the staff or rod of Jesse and the Bride who ascends from the desert with Mary. He explains that Mary, the wisp of smoke, is fragrant from aromatic spices because she is filled with the odors of virtue. He explicates the

[40] See below, p. 57.
[41] Honorius, *Expositio*, P.L., 162:403-404.
[42] Rupert of Deutz, *Commentaria in Cantica Canticorum*, P.L., 168:402.

desert as the journey from earth to heaven, through which the Bride, Mary, ascends, proceeding from virtue to virtue.[43]

The Prophecy of Isaias was used by medieval writers in dialectic, dramatic, and artistic forms in presenting the genealogy of Christ; and a discussion of the main terms of the Prophecy—the root, the staff, or rod, and the flower—occurs again and again in the commentaries, treatises, and sermons of the Fathers and exegetes of the Middle Ages. Jesse, the root, is the father of David, from whom the stem or rod, the Virgin, and the flower, Christ, both descended— the flower having come forth from the rod by the overshadowing of the Holy Spirit. Although the staff or rod was originally taken to symbolize Christ, as early as the third century Tertullian associates it with the Virgin and interprets the flower as Christ; this was the beginning of a long tradition asserting the same equation.[44]

The nine angels who speak the *laudes* each carry a lily which is the visual symbol of the verbal symbol of the Prophecy of Isaias. In medieval exegesis flowers signified different aspects of Mary's virtues: the rose, patience; the violet, humility; and the lily, chastity.[45] The lily is associated with the Prophecy of Isaias in the iconographical representations of the Jesse Tree in which the lily, the *fleur-de-lis*, is outlined in white, the central petal of each lily enclosing the royal ancestors. The medieval Christian found it natural to conjoin the royal motif with the heavenly Queen.

Of particular relevance here, since it shows how the Prophecy of Isaias relates to the general theme of the play, the movement

[43] Alanus de Insulis, *Elucidatio Compendiosa in Cantica Canticorum ad Laudem Deiparae Virginis Mariae, P.L.*, 210:74.

[44] Since the medieval mind attached such great value to the likeness of words, it has been frequently noted that the verbal similarity between *uirga* (rod, staff) and *uirgo* (Virgin) might account for the rod being interpreted as a symbol for Mary, but this comparison existed and held a certain currency for many centuries before a text explicitly calls attention to the similarity in sound between the two words. Probably not the first to do so, but typical of those who noted the phonological resemblance as being a reason for taking *uirga* to mean by interpretation *uirgo*, was Alanus de Insulis in *Liber Sentiarum, P.L.*, 210:246.

[45] Alanus de Insulis, *Elucidatio Compendiosa, P.L.*, 210:64. Philippe has the angels of the first rank carry lilies on green staves—the first rank a golden lily, the second rank an azure lily, and the third rank a silver lily. Earlier he indicated that green was symbolic of humility and blue of faith and hope. Bruno Signiensis, *Expositio in Exodus, P.L.*, 164:306, speaks of gold as wisdom and silver as purity.

from the Old Law to the New, is the fact that medieval exegetes often related the root of Jesse to the New Law of Love; for example, Alanus de Insulis says: "Behold the root of the Church is charity, about which it is said, 'A rod shall come forth from the root of Jesse.'"[46]

Another important point as far as the analysis of the play is concerned is that this passage depicts the essential spirit of the New Law in the seven-fold gift of the Holy Spirit—the seven spirits which constitute the Divine Essence, or the plenitude of grace. Often these gifts of the Spirit are ranked in ascending order, beginning with the fear of the Lord and mounting to wisdom, and classified as steps in the path of perfection.[47] And since from the beginnings of Christianity the Holy Spirit has been depicted in the form of a dove,[48] the foregoing meanings will have overtones for the dramatic action when Mary releases the dove in her hand at the end of the Play.

This seven-fold gift is also related to an image used by the second angel, that of the "Vessel of Divine Wisdom," which is used as a figure for Mary because her womb became the vessel which contained the Divine Wisdom, the Son of God. Alanus de Insulis, in explicating the passage, "Wisdom built herself a house, hewing out seven pillars" (Proverbs 9:1), gives three interpretations for "house," namely, the Virgin Mary, the Church, and the Body of Christ. He enlarges upon the idea: "'Wisdom,' who is God, 'built herself a house by hewing seven columns,' that is, by bestowing the seven gifts of the holy Spirit." These virtues, he says, are found in the soul of Mary or in any just soul, in the Church, and in Christ in plenitude.[49]

The metaphor "Vessel of Divine Wisdom" is closely related to another image used by the second angel, that of the "Ark of the Lord," and to one used by the fourth angel, that of the "Temple of God." All refer to the indwelling of the divinity in Mary and/or the Church. The eighth angel makes these metaphors explicit by saying that God will dwell in Mary. The ark and temple images point up the Old Law–New Law theme which we have already seen operating in the play. Ambrose, for example, speaks of David dancing before the Ark, and is immediately reminded that as the Ark of the Old Testament held the covenant of the Old Law, so Mary bore the

---

[46] Alanus de Insulis, *Sermo V: De Custodia Ecclesiae ad Sacerdotes in Synodo*, *P.L.*, 210:211.

[47] Herveus, *Commentaria in Isaiam*, *P.L.*, 181:140.

[48] See Matthew 3:16; Mark 1:10, Luke 3:22; and John 1:32.

[49] Alanus de Insulis, *Sententiae Allae*, *P.L.*, 210:261–262.

covenant of the New Testament within her.[50] Twelfth-century Bruno Signiensis contrasts the Ark of the Covenant with the bloody sacrifice of the New Law offered by the Church and points out that the Holy of Holies of Christ's humanity also resides in the Church where it is perpetually renewed in the New Covenant of the Eucharist.[51]

From the writings of the medieval exegetes, therefore, it can be discovered that from the profusion of images in the *Laudes Mariae*, central themes emerge. Earlier we saw that Mary's physical ascension of the steps represents a movement from virtue to virtue until perfect charity, the Spirit of the New Law, is reached. The Bride ascending through the desert is the allegorical journey of the soul traveling through this world, ascending the heights of virtue until she is united to Christ in the mystical marriage of the heavenly Jerusalem. The seven gifts of the Holy Spirit in the Prophecy of Isaias passage likewise represent steps in the path of perfection which constitute a plenitude of grace, the Spirit of the New Law. In all of these, Mary, the soul, and/or the Church is the Bride who moves from the Spirit of the Old Law, fear, to the Spirit of the New Law, charity, to enjoy the heavenly nuptials for all eternity.

Dramatic Encounters occurring between the Laudes Mariae and the Repraesentatio

ANNA AND JOACHIM

Music follows the *laudes* and then Anna and Joachim each in turn stand and speak. In the play's context Joachim and Anna are related to the Old Law–New Law theme—Joachim representing the period of preparation for the coming of the Redeemer under the Old Law, and Anna symbolizing the grace earned by Christ in his act of Redemption, the gift of the New Law.

The name Anna means "Grace" and she holds in her left hand

---

[50] *Sermones S. Ambrosio Hactenus Ascripti, P.L.*, 17:689: "But what shall we call the Ark unless Holy Mary? If indeed the Ark carried within itself the Tablets of the Testament, Mary bore the heir of that Testament itself, the former once for all within the law, the latter preserved the Gospel, the former had the voice of God, the latter the Word. Yet the Ark truly gleamed within and without with the brilliance of gold but holy Mary also glowed within and without with the splendor of virginity; the former [the Ark] was adorned with terrestrial gold, this one [Mary] with heavenly [gold]."

[51] See *Expositio in Exodum, P.L.*, 159:303–304.

the bread which signifies the spiritual grace of the New Law. The bread is the sacrament which is to be made fruitful in good works through the operation of the Holy Spirit. Anna's fruitfulness is stressed in the play when she stands and announces that God has done wondrous things for her, for she was sterile but bore a child who shall be an honor to the entire race. Anna is to be dressed all in white, signifying purity; the purification or the cleansing has already taken place and it is now time for the sacrifice and the good works which issue from it. Anna, then stands on the side of the New Law, for she is associated with producing the fruits of good works.

Joachim, whose name signifies "preparation for the Lord," is on the side of the Old Law and speaks as it were in the voice of a prophet. Joachim carries wine, which is the wine of the Mass, the Blood of Christ which cleanses the Church. Though at first it may seem enigmatic that an Old Testament figure, albeit an apocryphal one, should carry a symbol of the New Covenant, Joachim carrying the wine would be numbered among the members of the Old Law who eagerly anticipated the New Law which Christ would establish.[52]

Joachim's costume emphasizes his sacrificial role of preparer and purifier. Traditionally Joachim was a shepherd, and in most artifacts he is dressed like one. Philippe, however, requires that Joachim's attire be of a sacerdotal nature, that he be dressed in the manner of a priest. The whiteness of Joachim's garments suggests purification, the preparation for the New Law of charity.

Joachim, then, by virtue of his name, his emblem, and his attire, stands on the side of the Old Law, but in the same way that the prophets of the Tree of Jesse stand on the side of the Old Law, but anticipate the New. Joachim, being much later than the prophets, stands right at the dawn of the New Law of charity.

[52] Joachim's carrying the wine can be further clarified by an illustration from medieval sculpture. Chartres has ten statues of patriarchs and prophets arranged in chronological order, all prefiguring the coming of Christ; the last is Saint Peter, clad in dalmatic, crowned with the tiara, bearing the cross and chalice, announcing that Christ had fulfilled the prophecies, and that by creating the Church, he has established for all time the dominion of the New Testament. Emile Mâle, *Religious Art from the Twelfth to the Eighteenth Century* (New York: Noonday Press, 1958), p. 77, makes an observation concerning the symbolism of these statues which can be applied by analogy to Joachim and Anna in Philippe's play: "Each of the great figures of Chartres bears a symbol which announces Jesus Christ, which *is* Jesus Christ."

Ecclesia and Synagoga

The theme of the New Law which completes the Old Law is continued in Philippe's play by the two richly allegorical figures, Ecclesia and Synagoga. Each gives one speech which combined provide a sort of intervening episode between the speeches of Anna and Joachim and the dramatic action involving Michael and Lucifer.

As indicated earlier, Ecclesia is to be represented as being young, beautiful, and golden-crowned, carrying a cross and a sphere, while Synagoga is to be presented as elderly and shabbily dressed, with her eyes covered with a black cloth, carrying a banner with the arms of the Romans and two stone tablets on which are written the Law of Moses and the Old Testament. Ecclesia first speaks to Mary and then about Mary, and finally speaks of herself in language conventionally referred to Mary, so that the passage seems to refer to Mary and to the Church interchangeably. Thus Ecclesia establishes Mary as the first-fruit of the Church, and, as such, a type of all later children of Ecclesia, or as a figure of Ecclesia herself. In contrast, the desolate Synagoga speaks first of her own misery, and then indicates Mary as the one through whom truth will come. After her lament she is driven from the stage by Gabriel and Raphael, throws her banner and tablet off the platform, and flees wailing from the church.

The costumes, words, and actions of these allegorical figures held many implications for the medieval audience that witnessed Philippe's play, for an important body of church literature using them had originated with the Fathers of the Church to give tangible and concrete expression to the concept of the New Law which Christ brought to fulfill the Old Law.

The source of this highly interesting theme seems to be the pseudo-Augustinian dialogue, *De Altercatione Ecclesia et Synagogue*.[53] In this work Synagoga, represented as a widow, formerly rich and prominent but now deserted and abandoned, is dejected and discouraged; in contrast, Ecclesia is queenly and successful, boastful, and inclined to show her impatience with Synagoga for not accepting the truths of Christianity by hurling derogatory epithets. Ecclesia initiates the argument by stating that each will read what she considers important, to which Synagoga responds that all the prophets came to her. While

[53] *P.L.*, 42:1131–1139.

each cites authorities to support her claim to divine priority, and hence her claim to greater reverence, Synagoga merely mentions the prophets and Israel's claim as the chosen people, while Ecclesia's arguments are heavily laden with scriptural quotations, especially from the Old Testament. Like Ecclesia in Philippe's play, the pseudo-Augustine's Ecclesia argues that under the Old Law people are slaves, but under the New they are free. Despite Ecclesia's claims, Synagoga does not concede. Ecclesia, however, has the last speech, in which she establishes herself as triumphant.

Although there are many dialogues which form a link in the chain of this genre which extends over a thousand-year period,[54] one which constitutes an important link between the *Altercatio* and the medieval allegory of the figures is the "Disputatio Ecclesiae et Synagogae" now attributed to Gilbert of Tournai of the thirteenth century. This Synagoga has many similarities with her earlier prototype, but in the end she is convinced of the verities of the Christian faith and admits defeat. She concedes that she has been blind in her literalism and states that now her eyes have been opened so that she sees beneath the veil of the prophecies; the darkness has been illuminated. She then concludes with a prayer.[55]

The application of the Ecclesia-Synagoga symbolism inspired many first-rate works in the plastic arts; examples of this motif can be found in French, German, and Italian miniatures, paintings, stained-glass windows, ivories, tapestries, and sculptures. In the iconography of the Middle Ages the figure of Ecclesia, or the Church, remains fairly constant, being represented as a beautiful young girl, a crowned queen, who stands triumphant and composed, confident that she will carry off the victory. Her two invincible weapons, as in the play, are the cross and the chalice; Philippe adds to her emblems the gilt sphere, symbolizing the universal domination of the Church.

[54] For a comprehensive list of writings on the subject of Ecclesia and Synagoga, see Index 2, *P.L.*, 219, especially pp. 151–159, 666–686. See also Lukyne Williams, *Adversos Judaeos: A Bird's-Eye View of Christian Apologiae until the Renaissance* (Cambridge: Cambridge University Press, 1935).

[55] "Disputatio Ecclesiae et Synagogae," in *Thesaurus novus Anecdotorum*, ed. Edmond Martène and Ursin Durand (Paris, 1717), pp. 1497–1596. See also Margaret Schlauch, "The Allegory of Church and Synagogue," *Speculum* 14 (1939):455.

The iconography of Synagoga has been rich and varied. Although she is usually pictured with a bent or broken spear in one hand and the two tablets of stone slipping from the other, symbolizing that the reign of legalism has been superseded by the reign of charity, sometimes the knife of circumcision or the overturned chalice are used to individualize Synagoga in contrast to Ecclesia with the upright chalice and cross. Philippe gives Synagoga a red banner on which is written in letters of gold "S.P.Q.R." (*Senatus Populusque Romanus*), the insignia of Rome, as a reminder that the New Law replaces both the law of the pagan emperor and the Old Law, and suggesting that the effects of the New Law are to extend to both the sphere of Church and the sphere of Empire, in that the Synagogue became the Church and the pagan emperor became the Christian.

The obstinacy of the Jews in refusing to embrace Christianity and to accept baptism is most frequently characterized in the Fathers by the literary figure of *caecitas*—blindness, interpreted as literalistic understanding—as opposed to the light of the vision of truth. Reference was also made to the Lamentations of the Pseudo-Jeremiah (5:16) which states that "the crown is fallen from our head; our eyes are covered with a veil." From the figurative expression of blindness versus vision flowed the most consistent and conspicuous trait in delineating the allegorical figure of Synagoga, namely, the blindness of her literalism identified, as Philippe does in the play, by a cloth covering her eyes.

MICHAEL AND LUCIFER

Following the expulsion of Synagoga from the Church, Michael and Lucifer take the center of the stage for a brief interval. Although representations of Saint Michael in the Middle Ages were many and varied, he is usually depicted as young and beautiful, clothed in a dazzling coat of mail with shining sword, spear, and shield, similar to a medieval knight in shining armor, but with resplendent wings rising from his shoulders and sometimes wearing a jeweled crown. It is in this way that Philippe chose to represent Michael, and he indicates that the gilt crown symbolizes both a victorious soldier and Christ triumphant. Michael, whose name means *Quis ut Deus*, "Who is like God," is mentioned four times in sacred Scripture, twice in the Old testament and twice in the New; he is related to the New Law–Old Law theme, or the Ecclesia-Synagoga theme, for he is the champion of God's people, the Jews in the Old Law, the Christians in the New. Durand asserts that when the power of the Synagogue ceased and was replaced by the power of the Church so that the Christians became the people of God, then Michael, who had been the great prince of the Hebrew people, became the prince and leader of the Church Militant in Christendom.[56]

The New Testament passages concerning Michael both depict him as a warrior, the one being an allusion to the occasion "when Michael the archangel was fiercely disputing with the devil about the body of Moses" (Epistle of St. Jude, 1:9), and the other rendering a dramatic account of the battle in heaven: "Michael and his angels battled with the dragon, and the dragon fought his angels; and they did not prevail, neither was their place found any more in heaven. And that great dragon was cast down, the ancient serpent, he who is called the devil and Satan, who leads astray the whole world" (Revelation 12:7–9). Following these scriptural passages Christian tradition has given Michael certain offices, such as fighting Lucifer, rescuing the souls of the faithful from the power of the devil, especially at the hour of death, calling man's souls to judgment, and championing God's people. Durand adds another dimension to Michael's significance by asserting that while in a historical sense the devil was fought by Michael and the other angels, in an allegorical sense Michael signifies Christ; also, the battle signifies the persecution which the faithful suffer in the present Church, the Church Militant.[57]

In contrast to the handsomely garbed Michael, Lucifer in the play is to be as ugly as possible in appearance. As the *Rebellator Dei*, the archenemy of God, it is fitting that in the drama he should have either a hook in his right hand or an iron hook over his shoulder, a symbol of his attempt to ensnare souls.

The evolution of the diabolic motif in the history of mankind has been one of constant transformation, having progressed from a serpent, to a dragon, to a demon, and now in modern times, to a perfectly human person. The devil in Philippe's play does not go beyond the conventional bellowing and roaring of the Satanic characters in early religious drama. The frisky, tricky devil to whom we attribute much of the humor in medieval drama was to develop slightly later than the Presentation Play. Philippe directs that Lucifer,

[56] Durand, *Rational*, vol. 5, bk. 7, p. 56.
[57] Ibid., p. 58.

who has no speaking part, should howl loudly as he is dragged along by Michael.

When Michael and his prisoner ascend the platform, Lucifer is so frightened of the Virgin that he tries to hide his face. First Michael salutes Mary as the mightiest Queen whom all creatures of heaven, earth, sea, and abyss must obey, and then he proceeds to upbraid Lucifer for his rebellion against God and his enmity toward man.

Symbolically, the representation of Michael and Lucifer in the play as the power of light and the power of darkness at war, with Michael overcoming Lucifer and placing him in chains, is a foreshadowing of the final binding of Satan at the end of time described in Revelation. It signifies the power of the redemptive scheme of the New Law to overthrow Satan, the king of Babylon, and to establish the heavenly Jerusalem for all eternity.

Philippe directs that Michael should put Lucifer under Mary's feet so that she can trample on him; this symbolizes dramaturgically her overcoming of the devil. Lucifer is then expelled permanently by Michael, Gabriel, and Raphael, creating a kind of *visio pacis* which is to come after the Last Judgment.

The Dramatic Presentation

As the characters in the play form a procession to the altar for the dramatic portrayal of the presentation, the hymn *Veni creator spiritus* is sung. This relates to the seven-fold gift of the Spirit discussed earlier in the Prophecy of Isaias passage and, since the Holy Spirit is symbolized by a dove, to the flight of the dove from Mary's hands at the end of the play, which will be referred to later.

Anna addresses the Lord, asking him to accept Mary, the fruit wondrously conceived, and "chosen by you for His Habitation"—a phrase which echoes such imagery in the *laudes* as "Vessel of Divine Wisdom." Then Joachim, in his speech of oblation, pleads with the Lord to come quickly and enter the Virgin so that she may become a prophet for the faithful, and that through her humanity might be redeemed from Babylonian servitude. Babylon was traditionally associated with the left hand, the Old Law, and contrasted sharply with the right hand, Jerusalem, the New Law. Frequently a symbolic use of the two cities provided a contrast between evil and good, sinfulness and holiness, confusion and peace, cupidity and charity. The journey from Babylon to Jerusalem implied here was a common metaphor in the Middle Ages for the journey of the spiritual life of man.[58]

After Joachim and Anna present Mary to the bishop, who represents God the Father, he calls her in terminology from the Canticle: "Come my Beloved, come my Dove, because there is no spot on you. Come from Lebanon, my Chosen from eternity, that I might accept you as Bride for my beloved Son." The medieval interpretation of this passage indicates that the many levels of meaning attached to it are similar to those attributed to the earlier passage from the Canticle discussed in the *Laudes Mariae*.

Just as the arising from the desert in the previous text was taken to signify an ascent to perfection by preferring the spiritual concern to the material satisfaction for its own sake, so the Bridegroom's invitation that the Bride should come from Lebanon is interpreted as a call to the practice of virtue. Cassiodorus elaborated upon this concept of advancement in virtue, giving mystical significance to each time the Bridegroom invites the Bride, the soul, to come. According to his explication, the Bridegroom at the first call urges the Bride to come to the cleansing waters of baptism; the second call, to lay aside the chains of the flesh; the third call, to be perfect in thought, word, and deed. The first time he asks her to come through faith; the second time, to advance in virtue which leads to God; and the third time, to accept the crown and the joys of the "eternal nuptials."[59] Rupert states succinctly that the Bride is thereby to arrive at the theological virtues of faith, hope, and charity.[60]

Another viewpoint is expressed by Origen and his followers who explain this text as the call to Ecclesia, the Christian Church, to come forth. His interpretation sees Christ standing behind the wall of the house of the Old Testament, beginning to show himself to the Bride sitting within it, that is, within the letter of the Law, through the windows of the Law and the Prophets. But now she must come forth from the Old Law, the law of the Letter, to the New, the law of the Spirit.[61] The twelfth-century Bernard sees in

---

[58] This allegorical journey is specifically mentioned in the English play about the Presentation of the Virgin referred to earlier; immediately following the lines concerning the fifteen degrees which the soul must ascend the Bishop says: "Ffrom Babylony to hevynly Jerusalem this is the way."

[59] Cassiodorus, *Expositio in Cantica Canticorum*, P.G., 70:1075–1076.

[60] Rupert, *Commentaria in Cantica Canticorum*, P.L., 168:867.

[61] Origen, *Homilias in Canticum Canticorum*, P.G., 13:145.

this passage the three states to which the Church is called—preaching, prayer, and contemplation.[62]

Like the Prophecy of Isaias and the Ecclesia-Synagoga theme discussed earlier, this passage in the play involves a movement from the Old Law of the Letter to the New Law of the Spirit, from the concern for the corporeal to concern for the spiritual, from the active to the contemplative, from the earthly to the heavenly Jerusalem. The Bridegroom, seeing the beginning of virtue in the Bride, beckons her to cast aside all things corporeal and come to Him so that she may be united to him in eternal bliss. Though all of the exegetical references to this passage given here equate the Bride with the Church, we can assume that their echoes would apply to Mary, the Bride in this play, since she was, as we have seen, frequently identified with the Church.

Ending of the Play

Philippe concludes the play by having the bishop take the child Mary in his arms and hold her up to kiss the altar. Then Joachim and Anna offer their bread and wine on the altar and kiss it, leaving before it Mary and the two virgins, who are led by Gabriel and Raphael to the second platform prepared between the altar and the seats of the choir toward the northern side of the church. Mary and the virgins place their candles in the holders in front of them.

When the Mass is about to begin, Mary is to let fly her dove. This visual emblem of the moving dove is, in a sense, the externalization of the verbal image of the dove which is implied in the first angel's reference to the seven gifts of the Holy Spirit, and which reappears in the final speech, by the bishop, "Come my Dove." The dove which Mary carries is portrayed as being white, for white is the color in which all the virtues are symbolically united. According to early writers on symbolism, every virtue had its own emblematic color; and white, being produced by the blending or combination of all the seven prismatic hues, is with particular propriety employed as symbolic of that union of every virtue with the most exalted intelligence which exists in the person of the Holy Spirit.[63]

[62] Bernard, *Sermones in Cantica, P.L.,* 183:1054.
[63] Walafridus Strabo, *Glossa Ordinaria, P.L.,* 114:853, states that the Holy Spirit in the figure of a dove renders the concept that the Holy Spirit is dynamic in that he continues his operations.

As was stated earlier, the dramatic presentation of Philippe's play begins with the hymn to the Holy Spirit, *Veni creator spiritus*, asking him to come with his seven-fold gifts and guide minds with his light and to inflame hearts with his love. When, at the end of the play, the Virgin allows the dove to fly, the implication is that she will be overshadowed by the Holy Spirit and conceive thereby a divine Son. But an equally important significance of this action is that the Holy Spirit proceeds into the world with the Father and the Son in an eternal procession to sanctify souls.[64] It is Mary, the dove of the Canticle, who releases the dove, the Holy Spirit, by her consent to the divine Motherhood. On another level, it is the Church, who by the graces of the sacraments, releases the seven-fold gifts of the Holy Spirit.

When the Mass is finished, Mary descends the stage with the two virgins, kisses the altar, and offers her candle, the virgins doing likewise. The carrying of the candles and the offering of them are significant actions in Philippe's play. When he directs that the clergy also should carry lighted candles, and suggests that others in the procession would benefit by doing so also, he refers to this symbol as a new light from the womb which afterwards will illuminate the whole world. And previously, in the first paragraph, he had stated that the Virgin Mother is she with whom there is light, revealing the mysteries that are about to come.

Durand gives many reasons why people in processions should carry lighted candles. A major one is that, like the Wise Virgins of the parable, they will have oil in their lamps, the oil of good works, when the Bridegroom comes. Then they, the elect, will go before the Spouse and will enter the bridal chamber of the celestial city.[65] In recalling that Moses made seven lamps, Durand states that they represent the seven gifts of the Holy Spirit which are responsible for lighting the darkness of the world and for dissipating the darkness of our spiritual blindness,[66] a concept which can be linked to the "blindness" of Synagoga.

The candle, like the dove symbol, is to light the darkness of spiritual blindness. As the flame of the Holy Spirit is to inflame the hearts of men, so men are to light the darkness by the flame of their good works. And like the dove of the Canticle, the Wise Virgin, the

[64] Hugo of St. Victor, *De Sacramentis Christianae Fidei*, *P.L.*, 176:199.
[65] Durand, *Rational*, vol. 5, bk. 7, pp. 43–45.
[66] Ibid., vol. 1, bk. 1, p. 28.

faithful soul, will await the Bridegroom with lighted candle so as to enjoy a mystical marriage in the heavenly Jerusalem. In all of these things, as she did in her perfect cooperation with the workings of the Holy Spirit, Mary can serve as a model.

When, during the reading of the Gospel, Mary and the two virgins stand with their lighted candles, they create a correspondence between the visual and verbal symbol of the Word. After the Mass when Mary kisses the altar, the symbol of Christ, and offers the candle, a symbol of Christ illuminating the world, the dramatic presentation is completed.

But the celebration of the feast continues as Mary is carried around the city by a gentleman of noble stature, or rides a palfrey, accompanied by the angels on two other horses, weather permitting. Upon their return to the banquet hall, Mary is seated in a lofty place on a regal throne, served with diligent solicitude and profound reverence by Gabriel and Raphael.

III. Conclusion

As one searches for meaning in Philippe's Presentation Play, for the significance hidden beneath its visible words, actions, costumes, and setting, it becomes evident that the play itself and the commentary supplied by Philippe provide insights into how a general medieval aesthetic operates in one particular medieval drama as representative of its kind.

Philippe makes general claims about the efficacy of the feast in the Letter sent to all the Christians of the Western world, and he indicates the symbolic meaning of various aspects of his production in the text of the Presentation Play. But neither the Letter nor the commentary is adequate for a complete interpretation. The Letter refers to the feast rather than specifically to the drama, though, since the play might be said to be an elaboration of the feast, many of the statements in the Letter can also be applied to the play. The commentary which Philippe provides for the play is obviously incomplete and presupposes a knowledge of symbolic meaning; it never expresses as a coherent whole the idea contained in the play.

In this brief study I have tried to explicate the details not explained and to show that this explication supplies a rational and full context for the statements made in the Letter. I have discovered the missing components uniting general themes and specific details by a method of interpretation appropriate to the age in which the play was produced—namely, the exegetical interpretation of the Bible which ascribes levels of meaning to biblical language.

The primary explicit images of the play are the bridal imagery and the superseding of the Old Law by the New. There are also many images which may be elaborated as ascents and journeys and thus fortify the most dramatically impressive action in the play, Mary's ascent of the temple steps. The central concern of the play is man's coming to God. It sets forth the way in which Mary, the individual soul or the Church, moves from one state to another state, from the unconsecrated to the consecrated, from the active to the contemplative, from the material to the spiritual. It exhibits a spiritual journey through this early existence to the heavenly homeland: for Ecclesia, the Church, it is a journey from the Synagogue to Christianity to the heavenly kingdom; for Mary, it is the voyage from the Old Law to the New Law to the eternal nuptials; and for the individual soul, it is the pilgrimage from Babylon to the heavenly Jerusalem and eternity with the Beloved. The ascending steps of the seven gifts of the Holy Spirit of the Prophecy of Isaias, the ascending steps through which the Bride moves as she rises from the desert in the Canticle of Canticles, and the steps to the altar of the child Mary as she moves to the Gradual Psalms, all are symbolic of the purification necessary if man is to be capable of love and to respond to the New Law.

Mary is a useful symbol for all that Philippe means by the play, for she stands between the Old and New Law, at the beginning and end of the journey, the last of the Old and the first of the New. As a representative of the Church, or the souls within the Church, she incarnates the idea that anybody can give himself to God in the presentation of himself.

What was the experience of the drama like for the sophisticated observer at the Court of Avignon or the Court of Charles V? I have tried to reconstruct detail by detail what the individual figures meant, but this kind of exercise can never recover the spontaneous response to symbolism which comes from being thoroughly imbued in the symbolic expression of the culture. Nor would I claim that any one spectator saw all that I have discovered in my laborious elucidation of the mysteries in the play. But the explication of these various elements does establish, in a sense, the possibilities of meaning implicit in this kind of drama; some of it surely was recognized by many observers.

The offering of the Virgin Mary in the Temple in Philippe de Mézières's play is not a historical event, an event distant in time and place, nor an oblation made in Jerusalem many centuries before the fourteenth. It is such an offering of a life to God as any cleric or layman in the audience at Avignon in 1372, or, from Philippe's perspective, anywhere in the world at any point of time, might make to show his love to the God of love. The message requires the characters, dialogue, costumes, and emblems; these, in turn, require the interpretation of scriptural symbolism resting on the conventional practice of medieval exegetes.

M. CATHERINE RUPP, O.S.M.

College of St. Mary
Omaha, Nebraska

The Presentation Play

My object in this translation has been to make the items of particular interest— the details of production and the symbolic content—completely understandable in modern terms. My text thus indicates the materials, colors, and designs of costumes and stages, the gestures and movements of the players, and the methods of crowd control with enough clarity to be used as the basis of a contemporary production. The Latin text does not always allow for such clarity, and skeptics are invited to draw different conclusions. As for the symbolic content, I have tried to use English terms which correspond to the elements and ideas in the text even when these terms are not those of the most familiar translations of Scripture and the liturgy. In general I have used the Douay version of the Bible as the basis of my translation, since it is the nearest to the Vulgate which Philippe would have used. But I have departed from the Douay when its terms would seem to distort or misrepresent Philippe's meaning. In some cases I have had to resort to footnotes, as when Philippe's symbolism is dependent upon an untranslatable pun. He wishes a costume to be colored "celestina" but in English, there is no shade of blue called "heavenly."

The Latin text which follows the translation is reproduced from Karl Young, The Drama of the Medieval Church *(Oxford: Clarendon Press, 1933), 2: 227–242, without Young's editorial apparatus. The same text was earlier published by Young in PMLA 26 (1911): 181–234. His text is taken from the manuscript in the Bibliotheque Nationale (MS lat. 17330), written in Philippe de Mézières's own hand, which also contains other documents related to the feast of the Presentation. These documents are described and listed below, p. 49.*

An English translation of the Presentation Play was previously published in a limited edition: see Albert Weiner, Philippe de Mézières' Description of the Dramatic Office for the Feast of the Presentation of the Virgin Mary in the Temple, *translated, with an introduction on "The Rise of Modern Acting" (New Haven: Privately printed by Andrew Kner, 1958).*

3

The Presentation Play

Of certain acts representing the Presentation of the Blessed Mary in the Temple and of the procession to be made during the Mass[1]

To whatever persons are devoted to that Mother who gives wisdom to the wise and the discipline of knowledge to the intelligent, who reveals what is deep and hidden and knows those things established in darkness,[2] with whom the light is which reveals the mysteries to come, to whom descended that great and perfect gift for the benefit of all: it is pleasing to reveal that on the twenty-first day of November, in commemoration of that day on which this Mother of the Eternal Word went to be presented by her parents of the flesh at the temple of the Lord in order that she might be present where to serve is to reign perpetually, those who are spotless according to their vows[3] have ordained a certain solemnity accompanied by the representation

[1] This title appears in the manuscript, not as a heading for the Presentation Play, but as an item in the table of contents. It is reproduced in Young, *Drama of the Medieval Church*, 2:472, and reads as follows: "De quibusdam actibus representantibus eandem Presentationem Beate Marie in Templo et processione fienda in Missa."

[2] "And he ... giveth wisdom to the wise, and knowledge to them that have understanding. He revealeth deep and hidden things, and knoweth what is in darkness; and light is with him" (Daniel 2:21–22, where the action is ascribed to God).

[3] These spotless persons are here kept deliberately ambiguous. George La Piana believes they are the early Fathers of the Church ("The Byzantine Iconography of the Presentation of the Virgin Mary to the Temple and a Latin Religious Pageant," in *Late Classical and Mediaeval Studies in Honor of Albert Mathias Friend, Jr.* [Princeton: Princeton University Press, 1955], pp. 264–265). Philippe apparently wanted to leave the founding unexceptionable, if indefinite in time; his reference could apply as well to those who approved his feast at Avignon. See the Letter, below, pp. 52, 58.

of most devout words, new acts, and ornate signs.[4] By this means they declare to all believing in Christ that through this most humble presentation of the Virgin in the temple all catholic fundamentals had their beginning; by this means also the mind, released from the weight of the flesh, may be enabled to arrive at knowledge of the invisible and visible elements of God's mysteries as it were through visible things, signs, and works, in accord with apostolic teaching.[5] This is lucidly set forth in the following order:

First: the twenty-two persons required for the performance of the representation, along with their names.

Second: their costumes and various ornaments.

Third: how to set up the place for the whole representation.

Fourth: the performance and order of the procession.

Fifth: the performance of the representation and of the *laudes*.

Sixth: the Mass to be celebrated for the feast of the Presentation, along with a brief sermon.

First of all, there will be a certain very young and very beautiful virgin of around three or four years of age, who represents Mary, and along with her two other most beautiful virgins of the same age. Then there will be Joachim and Anna; besides, there will be two angels, Gabriel and Raphael. Then there will be nine angels standing for the nine orders of angels. After this there will be a certain very beautiful woman[6] of about twenty, who is called Ecclesia, and stands for the Church. Then there will be a certain woman of advanced age, who will be called Synagoga, and will stand for the law of Moses and the Old Testament. Besides these, there will be two young

---

[4] Or "words, movements, and gestures." Philippe wishes to show the total care which the founders of this celebration devoted to its performance.

[5] This teaching is contained in Romans 1:20.

[6] Below, under costumes and ornaments, Philippe specifies that the part of Ecclesia will be played by an attractive and beardless young *man* with a wig coming down over his shoulders. It is quite possible that Synagoga and Anna were also played by men who were dressed in the manner described for them. In Latin, Philippe need not refer to Ecclesia with any pronoun; and when she must have a pronoun, it is feminine in agreement with the gender of Ecclesia. For the sake of convenience, the feminine pronoun will be supplied in this text, referring to the character Ecclesia rather than to the (male) actor.

6

men with stringed instruments. Next there will be Michael the archangel and Lucifer. Lastly there will be the bishop, with a deacon and a subdeacon.

The names of the persons in the representation having been listed, their costumes and ornaments will now be described

Mary will be dressed in a very white tunic of sendal,[7] without any superfluous artifice, with a small fold showing outside around the lower hem of the tunic. The tunic should be loose everywhere except in the sleeves, which should be tight, and she should not wear a belt around the tunic. Next she should put on a mantle, also very white, of sendal or of silk muslin, open in the front for the length of her body, with a little cord of gold thread tied in front to hold on the mantle, after the manner of a bridal mantle. Around the collar of the tunic and along the opening of the mantle should be sewn a little gold frieze, and around the bottom hem of the mantle there should also be a fold showing outside the mantle. Mary's head should be bare, and her hair should fall back over her shoulders. She should also wear on the top of her head a circlet of gold decorated with silver, about the width of a finger, along with a diadem of moderate width, decorated with silver, carefully fastened around the back of her head. Such will be the ornamentation for Mary's head. She should not wear rings or a girdle or anything else unless of white and gold, demonstrating the purity and virginity of Mary and the brightness of her charity.

As for the two virgins who will accompany Mary: one of them will be dressed in green silk or sendal, figuring Mary's humility, and the other in a blue or azure color, figuring Mary's faith and hope; for according to the apostle,[8] our conversation, but Mary's to a greater extent, is in heaven. These two virgins will not wear a mantle as Mary does, but they should wear the loose tunics with a fold around the lower hem described above. They also should not have any ornamentation on their tunics. On their bare heads they should wear circlets of silver, as described above, but not the diadems

[7] Sendal seems to have been a finer weave than ordinary silk, though the distinction between the two kinds of silk is now difficult to establish.

[8] "But our conversation [i.e., companionship] is in heaven, from which also we eagerly await a Savior" (Philippians 3:20). The symbolism here is based upon the Latin term *celestina*, for "celestial" or heavenly blue.

7

at the back. And their hair should hang down behind as was specified above concerning Mary.

As for Joachim, Mary's father, he will be dressed in a priest's alb, tied at the top like a priest's, with a stole around his neck extending across his chest in the form of a cross, as does a priest's. Over this he should wear an old-style unbroken *pluvialis*.[9] On his head he should wear a delicate and rather long, and, if such can be found, rather elaborate, piece of cloth, with which he should wrap his head and neck. The two ends of the cloth, about the length of two palms or a little more, should be thrown over his shoulders, right and left, over the *pluvialis*. In front he should wear a long, thick white beard hanging down over his chest, and he should carry in his hand, outside the *pluvialis*, a medium-sized glass cup filled with red wine.

Anna should be dressed in white linen, covering both her body and her head, in the manner of an honest matron of antiquity, and she should carry in her hand a round loaf of bread, as white as possible and rather large.

The two angels, Gabriel and Raphael,[10] should be dressed in white vestments wrapped at the top with stoles around the neck crossed in front of the chest. On their heads, they should wear birettas[11] fastened around the head above the ear. Around the head and on the top these should have the form of not very wide triangles or quadrangles, and should have two flaps behind like a bishop's miter. These birettas should be made out of white sendal or silk cloth, or out of papyrus or parchment, and should have little friezes with a design sewn around them, and pictures of flowers scattered over them. As well, whoever might like to could place behind the birettas little fringes of varicolored silk. The two angels should also

---

[9] The *pluvialis* (literally, "raincoat") was a poncho-like outer garment which had been largely replaced in the fourteenth century by the *alb*, the white garment still worn by a priest over the chasuble but under the outer garment colored according to the appropriate liturgical season. Joachim's wearing of the *pluvialis* may have made him seem like the old-fashioned priest which, according to legend, he had been.

[10] Gabriel and Raphael are traditionally and in this play designated as Mary's servants because Gabriel was the angel of the Annunciation (Luke 1:17) and Raphael was the angel who protected Tobit's wife from violation by lust (Tobit 3:17, *passim*).

[11] Birettas are tall peaked hats, which can be made stiff so as to stand up, and thus resemble the traditional bishop's miter.

8

have on two wings each, and they should each carry in the right hand a red staff.[12]

The nine angels should be dressed like Gabriel and Raphael, except that the three who represent the highest orders of angels, the cherubim and so forth, will wear birettas colored red, as described above, while the three of the second rank should have birettas of a blue or azure color, and the three of the third rank of angels, white birettas. All nine orders should carry lilies on delicate green-colored staves, with the lilies of the first orders, gold, those of the second orders colored azure, and of the third, silver.

Ecclesia will be played by some attractive young man of about twenty without a beard, and will be dressed in a deacon's habit, entirely of gold, with the hair of a most beautiful woman hanging down over the shoulders. On her head she will wear some sort of golden crown set with lilies and precious stones. Attached with a small cord in front of her chest will be a silver and gold chalice without any paten,[13] which chalice signifies the New Testament.[14] In the left hand she will carry a long cross, as wide as her body; and the top of this cross should be a red staff highly polished for its whole width, while the whole cross should be gilded and without any ornamentation. In the right hand she will carry a round ball, entirely gilded, signifying the universal dominion of the Church.

Synagoga will be dressed in the style of an old woman of antiquity with a worn-out tunic reaching to the ankles made of some kind of plain-colored cloth, and a torn, black mantle. Her head, in the style of an old woman, should be covered with a veil of a dark color, and she should wear a black veil in front of her face and eyes, though

---

[12] The word *virga* in Latin may be variously translated "branch," "rod" (as in Jesse's rod or Aaron's rod), or "staff." The angels carry these as symbols of their authority, so that the term should properly be translated "staff." But the pun on *virga-virgo* is important, if subdued, in the Presentation Play. Furthermore, the staves carried by the other angels, which have lilies at their ends, are clearly supposed to resemble living branches.

[13] The paten is the flat covering or plate carried by the priest and used to cover the chalice during Mass. Ecclesia's chalice is not specifically that used in Mass; it is rather that referred to by Christ as the sign of his new covenant.

[14] "In a like manner he took also the cup after the supper saying, 'This cup is the new covenant in my blood, which shall be shed for you'" (Luke 22:20; 1 Corinthians 11:25).

9

she should be able to see through it.[15] And in her left hand she should carry a reddish banner whose black staff appears to be broken, with the banner draped over her shoulder. On this red banner there should be written in letters of gold, "S.P.Q.R.," which are the arms of the Romans.[16] And in her right hand she should carry two stone tablets inclined towards the earth, on which tablets should be engraved letters looking like Hebrew letters, signifying the law of Moses and the Old Testament.[17]

The two youths who will play the sweet instruments will be dressed like the angels, except that they will not wear stoles or wings, but definitely will wear birettas of a green color.

Then there will be Michael the archangel, who will be armed with splendid armor from his feet to his head, and above his helmet or basinet or visor[18] he will wear some sort of gilded crown as the sign of victorious soldiers and as a sign of Christ triumphant. Also, in his right hand Michael will hold a naked sword, shining and held up towards heaven; and in his left hand he will hold an iron chain, on which Lucifer, tied at the neck, will follow behind Michael.[19]

Lucifer will be decked out with those ornaments which themselves befit what is most shameful and abominable, with horrible horns, teeth, and face. And in his right hand Lucifer will hold some kind

[15] Her ability to see through the veil is a stage direction only. This veil is that referred to by St. Paul: "We do not act as Moses did, who used to put a veil over his face that the Israelites might not observe the glory of his countenance, which was to pass away. But their minds were darkened; for to this day, when the Old Testament is read to them, the selfsame veil remains, not to be lifted to disclose the Christ in whom it is made void. Yes, down to this very day, when Moses is read, the veil covers their hearts; but when they turn in repentance to God, the veil shall be taken away" (2 Corinthians 3:13–16).

[16] In the Pseudo-Augustinian *Altercatio Synagogae et Ecclesiae*, Synagoga claims to have power over the Roman Empire (*Patrologia Latina*, 42:1131). This is an indication that Synagoga stands not so much for the Jews as a people, but for those principles of earthly domination represented equally by the Old Testament Israelites and the Imperial Romans.

[17] Letters written on tablets of stone are contrasted by St. Paul with the letters of Christ, written with the spirit (2 Corinthians 3:3, 3:7).

[18] Philippe allows his costumier here to use whatever kind of headgear is available. The *galea*, *bachinetum*, or *barbuta* were three kinds of helmets, the one covering the top and back of the head, the second, the face, and the third, the chin and front of the neck as well.

[19] Michael's victory over Satan, the basis for his role here, is recorded in Apocalypse 12:7–9.

of trundling hook or barbed hook of iron carried over the shoulder; and with his left hand he will hold the chain, as if trying to rebel against Michael.

In what manner the place for the performance of the play should be prepared

In the church between the great west door and the entrance to the choir for the canons or brothers, in the middle of the church, but a little nearer the choir entrance than the west door, so that it can be seen more clearly from all parts of the church, let there be constructed a wooden edifice or platform about six feet high, in the form of a balcony, which platform will extend across the width of the church, that is going north and south, about ten feet, and east and west about eight feet in width; and opposite the middle of the platform toward the west doors there will be stairs from the pavement of the church to the platform, and similar stairs opposite the entrance to the choir, for descending from the platform, in such a way that each stair will be about three feet long so as not to extend the platform very far; and these stairs, on either side, will be enclosed by boards or a wood railing so that no one will be able to climb them except in the order at the performance. On the top of the platform the floor will be level on the runway between the two sets of stairs; but towards the northern edge there will be a bench set up for sitting higher than the platform, extending from west to east, and this bench will be long enough for Joachim and Anna to be able to sit on either side with Mary in the middle, slightly elevated in the place where Mary sits so that her head will appear to be on a level with her father's and mother's when they are seated. And between the bench and the northern edge of the platform a space will be left for Gabriel and Raphael, who will stand behind Mary. There will be two seats on the southern part of the platform next to the steps as high as the bench upon which Joachim and Anna will sit, one seat on the eastern and one on the western side of the platform, where Ecclesia and Synagoga will sit facing Mary, but set back so that anyone coming up the stairs will be able to move freely between Ecclesia and Synagoga to the southernmost part of the platform. As for the four corners of the platform, Gabriel and Raphael will stand in the north corners and the two musicians in the south corners. All around, the platform will be protected with some thin boards extending about two feet above the platform in the manner of a podium, so that the said platform will appear more suitable for the performance of the representation, and so that those who are on the platform will not easily fall off. The platform, bench, and seats should be covered with tapestry. Let the strongest boards be used in the construction of the platform, and let it be well put together so that the weight of the people standing on it will not be enough to make it cave in.

Besides this, let another platform be constructed in some prominent place between the seats for the canons or brothers in the choir and the high altar, towards the north side and next to the door or a pillar, also of wood and higher but smaller than the other, that is, about seven or eight feet high. This platform will be a six-foot square on top, with a railing aroung it about a foot above the level of the platform within the square. And this platform will also be covered in tapestry, with a small footstool near the middle of the tapestry covered with fine silk, with a little silk cushion for Mary to kneel on while listening to the Mass. And right in the middle of the platform will be placed a larger silk cushion for Mary to sit on, with the aforesaid stool directly in front of her.

In addition, fix up a small room somewhere near the church, perhaps on the grounds, large enough to be used as a dressing room or place of preparation for the cast of the representation, the brothers' chapter house being the most likely place if closed off temporarily by curtains from some house near the church suitable for the purpose, so that our most sweet Mary and her companions may be readied, and, after being dressed and readied according to the instructions given above, may wait for the start of the procession.

Of the procession and its order

The bishop or the archbishop who is going to celebrate the Mass, dressed in pontifical robes and carrying his crosier,[20] with the deacon and subdeacon and other clergy preceding, carrying the priestly vestments and the reliquary of the high altar, will lead the procession singing in a loud voice, "Hail, O Queen,"[21] and the procession will go directly to the place where Mary is waiting, singing the whole way. And when the whole procession has reached this place or the chapter

[20] The crosier is the sign of the bishop's office, being in the form of a crooked shepherd's staff.

[21] For the text and translation of the popular hymn *Salve Regina*, see Appendix I.

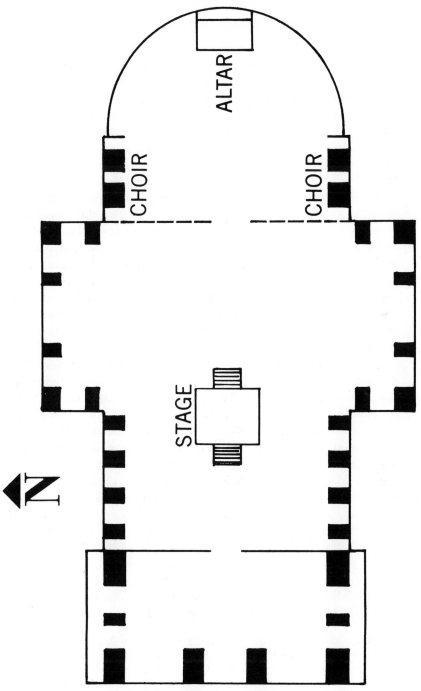

Location of Platform in Church

house, the bishop having passed by, the doors or curtains will be opened. One of the orders of angels will come out first with a white staff in his right hand as if to point out and clear the way, and this angel will fall in immediately after the bishop, about two steps behind him, so that no person will be able to get in between the bishop and the angel; the angel following the bishop in step will with his staff clear the way to the right and left. After this angel the other eight angels will follow, one after the other in gradations according to their ranks, the order of cherubim and seraphim slightly behind, carrying in the left hand the lily described above. Synagoga follows immediately after the nine angels, her head bowed, and carrying the banner and stone tablets mentioned above. And after Synagoga, Ecclesia will follow gracefully with her cross, the chalice next to her chest, and the gold ball in her right hand. The two musicians follow immediately after Ecclesia, marching together and striking their instruments. After the musicians the two virgins will come marching together, and she who is dressed in green will carry a candle of about one-third of a pound in her right hand, also green, and the other virgin similarly an azure candle.

Our most sweet Mary will follow immediately after the two virgins, carrying in her right hand a candle of the same weight, although of the whitest color, and she will hold against her breast in her left hand a certain very white dove; and Gabriel will march on Mary's right side, holding up his red staff; and Raphael will march even with her in a similar manner on the left side, respectfully, never approaching the person of Mary, but looking constantly toward her.

After Mary, Gabriel, and Raphael will come Joachim and Anna walking side by side and carrying their bread and wine as described above, and looking continuously at Mary. The archangel Michael will come after them armed with his sword, shining and erect, in his right hand, and drawing Lucifer on a chain with his left hand about one step behind him with much howling and cackling to indicate his unwillingness to come.[22]

After Mary has come out from the chapter house or other place where she has been waiting for the procession, one of the angels will

[22] It is expected that the actor playing Lucifer, as well as the one playing Synagoga, will be sufficiently comic to draw laughter from the crowd; later Philippe allows time for the hilarity of the audience to abate before the performance can continue. Even here, Lucifer is to be a figure of fun; the celebration of this feast is not to be uniformly solemn.

immediately place himself between the two musicians marching in the procession,[23] and begin to sing a song in a loud voice, to the playing of the instruments, a rondel[24] in praise of the Most Blessed Virgin, and let this song be in the vulgar tongue so as to excite the people to devotion. All of the angels, along with Ecclesia, Gabriel and Raphael, and the musicians, will join in the responses. The clergy, who up to this point had been singing the "Hail, O Queen," when they hear the Angel begin to sing will be silent, and all others will be silent except the angels, who will continue to sing the said rondel, one beginning and the others responding, proceeding in order until reaching the platform constructed in the middle of the church.

After Michael and Lucifer, the nobles and chief people will march, and afterwards other people of both sexes. The procession will go through the cloister up to the door which leads to the courtyard before the great doors to the west of the church. Here they will make a kind of circuit, turning around in this courtyard and returning to the great door of the church, marching and singing as above, until they reach the aforesaid platform. And note that each member of the clergy marching in the procession will carry a lighted candle in his hand, and if the nobles and other people wish to carry candles also while marching, in honor of that Light which is to come from the womb later to illuminate the whole world, do not by any means discourage them from carrying this light. Moreover, when Mary comes out of the chapter house with her companions, there will be certain able-bodied young men stationed outside, who will hold in their hands spear handles, and they will line up opposite each other for the length of the procession from the bishop to Lucifer, and stay on both sides marching with the procession, so that Mary and her companions in their adornments will not be jostled and will

[23] This angel will have to drop back behind Synagoga and Ecclesia to reach this position, thus constituting a break in the procession as described above. He will then be standing behind those who are to sing the responses in the rondel.

[24] The rondel is a verse form which has three stanzas, with a repetition of lines from the first stanza following the second and third, and with the rhymes of the first stanza carrying over in the second and third. The stanzas themselves, without repeated material, are usually of three lines, so that a typical rondel will have the form abb, abR, abbR, where R stands for the repetition of a line or lines from the first stanza, and a and b are rhymes. Chaucer's triple rondel "Youre eyen two wol sley me sodeynlye" is an English example.

have their way cleared for them by marching between the spears.[25] The men holding the spears will face towards the people outside the spears on either side as they march along, holding the people back with the spears so that no one may enter between the rows of spears except Mary and her companions, although there may be three or four servants or sergeants of justice inside the spears to allay the pressure of the people, lest Mary and her companions should be crushed by the people.

When the procession has entered the church, the bishop, with the members of the clergy, will cross alongside the platform and go to the high altar to his seat where he will sit during the performance of the representation along with the clergy, and afterwards during the Presentation of Mary which is to be made to the bishop himself. And Mary with her companions will stand still between the spear-holders in front of the platform which has been constructed, between the platform and the west door, the angels continuing their singing, until the bishop can get to his chair and all the people enter the church. Note that the procession ought to begin rather shortly after sunrise, because the mystery to be represented is long and most devout, and the days are short at this time.[26]

Of the performance of the representation and the laudes for Mary

The representation is in this manner. Gabriel and Raphael, with Mary, Joachim, and Anna, approach the foot of the stairs to the platform, the musicians preceding them and playing, while the other angels, Ecclesia, Synagoga, Michael, and Lucifer remain fixed in

[25] This direction, and probably the one requiring the little circuit before entering the church, assume the excited involvement of the crowd in the whole procession. These able-bodied men, besides being useful in crowd-control, may also, according to La Piana, be a vestige of the Byzantine iconography which had sixty angels accompany Mary to the temple ("Byzantine Iconography," pp. 269–270). La Piana suggests that they were stripped of their wings, these being difficult to wear in a crowd, and given the function of protecting their charge against physical rather than spiritual dangers.

[26] This statement and another to the same effect (see p. 28 below), indicates that the performance of the Presentation Play, the office of the feast, and the sermon would have taken longer than the text itself would lead us to believe, since Philippe seems worried that the whole celebration will take longer than the at least nine hours of daylight which he could use, in Avignon or Venice, on November 21.

their positions and waiting. The ascent of the stairs to the platform will be carefully supervised by the armed servants or the sergeants at arms in case some people presume to go up who are not to be in the performance of the representation. Gabriel shall ascend first to the platform, and, with his rod, will impose silence on all by turning to all sides gesturing without a word with his staff. And at once Mary, alone, will ascend the steps to the platform, with a joyous face, and without assistance. If she is unable to carry her candle while ascending, Raphael will hold it, and Mary will clutch her dove to her bosom while ascending, the instruments playing all the while. When Mary is standing on the platform with her face toward the great altar, Raphael will go up at once, and he along with Gabriel will usher Mary to her seat toward the northern side, as described above. And then Gabriel and Raphael together will do obeisance to Mary with deep reverence, and will go in back of her, Gabriel to the corner of the platform toward the east standing up and looking constantly at Mary with his rod held up, and likewise Raphael to the other corner of the platform behind Mary with his rod erect. Mary will hold the dove with both hands to her breast, sometimes kissing it and pressing it to her bosom. And Mary's candle will be placed by Raphael in the candlestick in front of Mary; and likewise when they have come up, the two candles of the two virgins will be placed on the platform in two candlesticks on a line with Mary's. Then the two virgins will go up the stairs together holding their candles, and will seat themselves at Mary's feet. Afterwards the two musicians will ascend and station themselves in the corners of the platform toward the southern edge, each in his own corner, looking at Mary and playing. Right after the musicians climb up, Joachim and Anna will ascend, and with their heads slightly bowed as if in reverence for Mary, will sit on the bench described above, Mary in the middle facing the front towards the south edge, Joachim to Mary's left towards the east, and Anna sitting on her right towards the west. And immediately Synagoga will ascend and after her Ecclesia, and they will sit on the stools described earlier, that is, Synagoga on the eastern side and Ecclesia on the western, looking at Mary, and Synagoga carrying a banner and tablets, and Ecclesia a cross and ball, as is declared above. There will be an open way between the two stairs to the platform, between the ascent to the platform to the west and the descent on the east and between Mary, Joachim, and Anna sitting on a line, and Gabriel and Raphael standing behind in the corners of the platform on the north end, and between Synagoga and Ecclesia, with the musicians standing back in the south corners of the platform and playing.[27]

Coming now to the *laudes* for Mary: after Gabriel and Raphael have imposed silence with their staves, the first angel, who holds a white staff in his right and a lily in his left hand, will climb on to the platform with his staff erect; and when he comes before Mary, he will put his staff on the tapestry and bow low to Mary, and then place himself between Synagoga and Ecclesia and the musicians holding their instruments, with his face turned towards Mary, and, holding the lily up with his left hand before all the church, and with his right hand pointing to Mary, will begin to chant in a loud voice as if singing:

> Who is she who ascends from the desert as a wisp of smoke, from the fragrance of myrrh and frankincense: is it not that staff which will arise from the root of Jesse, and will not a flower come forth from that root, and the spirit of the Lord rest on him, the spirit of wisdom and knowledge, the spirit of learning and counsel, the spirit of piety and courage, and the spirit of the fear of the Lord?[28]

This having been said, the instruments will play, and this angel will come before Mary and, bowing before her, will pick up his staff and descend from the platform by the east stairs, then place himself between the steps and the opening to the choir, where the able-bodied young men holding spears in two opposite rows, as was described above, will station themselves to receive both the angels and Mary when they come down from the platform as well as when they will go through the choir to the high altar for the presentation of Mary to the bishop. After the first angel has come down from the platform, the instruments still playing, the second angel will go up to the plat-

---

[27] As Illustration 2 shows, these directions bring all the players onto the stage except the nine angels and Michael and Lucifer. These will ascend the stairs one at a time to deliver their lines.

[28] "Who is this who ascends from the desert as a wisp of smoke, laden with myrrh, with frankincense" (Canticles 3:6); "And there shall come forth a stem out of the root of Jesse, and a flower shall rise up out of this root. And the spirit of the Lord shall rest upon him, the spirit of wisdom, and of understanding, the spirit of counsel and of fortitude, the spirit of knowledge, and of godliness. And he shall be filled with the spirit of the fear of the Lord" (Isaias 11:1-3). Note that in the Latin a "wisp" (*virgula*) is the diminutive of a "stem" or "rod" (*virga*).

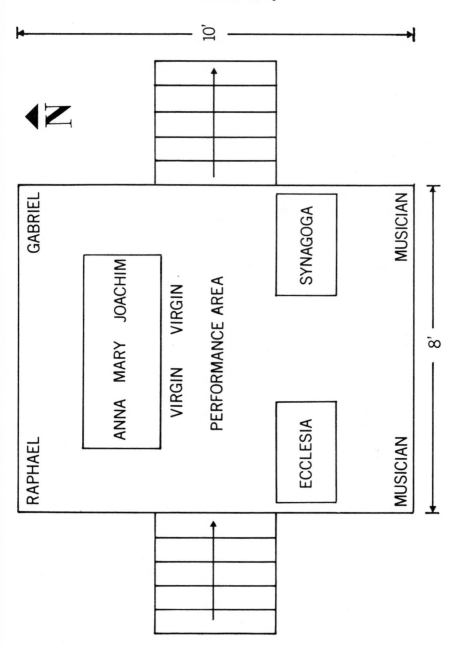

Location of Players on Platform

form by the west stairs and, with his lily in his left hand, bow low to Mary, then take the same position as the other angel between Ecclesia, Synagoga, and the musicians. Still holding the lily up with his left hand, and extending his right toward Mary, he will chant in a loud voice,

Behold, our joy approaches,

with his hands turning to the right and to the left, and returning to Mary he chants:

Look forth and see the beautiful Virgin, pleasing to God, shining in brightness, giving joy to angels, persevering in honesty, and adorning the world. Day of immense joy and great exultation to all creatures! for behold the Ark of the Lord, the Vessel of Divine Wisdom and the Salvation of Shipwrecked Nature, who is today presented in the temple, dedicated to God and pledged forever to the honor of Almighty God.

Which being said, the instruments will play and the angel bow himself toward Mary and descend like the first angel, and take his place waiting. The third angel will go to the same position and chant:

The Virgin ascends to the temple, and angels descend to her. She is called a handmaiden and will become a lady; is called humble and will humble God; vows to be a virgin and will bring forth God. You are the Virgin, the example to virgins, the Woman who is the model for women, the Lady who is the standard for ladies; you are blessed because through you the virgins are graced, the women are blessed, and all saints are rewarded through you.

The fourth angel says:

Behold Virginity, behold Humility, behold Gentleness, behold Purity, behold Innocence, behold perfect Charity, in whom dwells immense Goodness, and behold she who will be made the Bride, Mother, and Temple of God.

And it will be noted that all of the angels chant or sing their verses or songs in the same place, and after climbing onto the platform, stand and sing bowed before Mary, and in descending from the platform and in waiting between the east steps of the platform and the entrance to the choir they will keep that order which has been set forth above for the first two angels. The fifth angel will sing saying:

O Great Edifice, in which will be sustained human fragility, over which will be built the universal faith, from whom will go forth perfect virginity, and in whom will be gathered back immense goodness; from you, through you, and in you the highest divinity will be praised.

The sixth angel will sing and say:

O admirable Lady in the sight of man, in the sight of angels, and in the presence of God! Who is worthy to praise you, who is worthy to call upon you, since in the world you are without a peer, and in nature without a stain, and in heaven you shall be with immense glory?

The seventh angel will sing and say:

Hail, our Lady, hail the Reparation of Human Nature, hail the Mediatrix of Divine Justice and she in whom the mercy of God will be shown, because you will be mother and virgin, God and man, faith and the human heart. Surely wonderful was the climbing up of the girl in her climb, but more wonderful the working of the girl in her wisdom, yet most wonderful the bending down of God in his descent, which shall be a joy to the holy Fathers and to all who love God, because we shall rejoice with her before God through infinite worlds without end.

The eighth angel will chant or sing:

Hail, Mary, full of grace, the Lord is with you;[29] and more with you than in heaven, for in you he will dwell, assuming from you his flesh; he shall be with you and with all who are with you, who love you, who honor you; with you the Creator will be. O creature of the Lord, O handmaid of the Bridegroom, O admirable Bride, we bless you, we praise you, we adore you, through infinite worlds without end.

The ninth angel from among the cherubim will sing saying:

O inestimable love! O immeasurable devotion! O infinite charity!

while pointing to himself with his hand; then, pointing to Mary with his hand, he says:

Behold her to whom will be given the price of human redemption, the gift of infinite value, and the reward of the highest perfection!

[29] Luke 1:28.

21

Here is that Virgin, the humble Mother of the Son of God, who will be overshadowed by the Holy Ghost,[30] be called the chosen among handmaidens, and be rewarded in the company of God the Father in eternity.

The instruments still playing, and the nine angels in their positions as they marched in the procession waiting on the floor between the platform and the entrance to the choir, Anna the mother of Mary will rise and stand in her place; the instruments having been quieted, she will raise both of her hands to heaven with the bread in the left, and in the heavy voice of a woman widowed and aged will say:

> Listen, sons of Israel, exulting with me, because a miracle of God I will tell: the sterile is made mother (*pointing to herself with her hand*), and exultation is born in Israel. Behold, I may offer a gift to the Lord, and my enemies cannot prevent me. The Lord God has made the memory of his words into a deed, and he has visited his people with the visitation of his grace.[31]

Having said this and kissed Mary, she will sit in her place, as before, and the instruments will play softly. Then Joachim will rise and stand in his place, and similarly will raise his hands to heaven with the wine in his left, and turning himself to the right and left gesturing with his hands will say in a loud voice:

> Rejoice all women, because your shame will be erased; and you all men, because God will be born as a man from her (*pointing to Mary with his hands; then turning himself to the angels*); and you all angels, because your seats are to be restored.

[30] "And the angel answered and said to her, 'The Holy Spirit shall come upon thee and the power of the Most High shall overshadow thee; and therefore the Holy One to be born shall be called the Son of God'" (Luke 1:35).

[31] Anna's speech is adapted from the *Gospel of the Pseudo-Matthew*, where she is reported to have said, on the occasion of her daughter's presentation: "The Lord God of Hosts hath been mindful of His word, and hath visited His people with a good and holy visitation, to bring down the Gentiles and turn their hearts to Himself. He hath opened His ears to our prayers: He hath kept away from us the exulting of our enemies. The barren hath become a mother, and hath brought forth exultation and gladness to Israel. Behold the gifts which I have brought to offer to my Lord, and mine enemies shall not be able to hinder me" (Sister Mary Jerome Kishpaugh, *The Feast of the Presentation of the Virgin Mary in the Temple: An Historical and Literary Study* [Washington: Catholic University of America, 1941], pp. 6–7).

Then he will turn himself every which way and say:

And you all creatures, because through her you shall be adorned.

And with hands raised to heaven, genuflecting, his face toward the north part where he was sitting, he will conclude, saying:

Let us all therefore rejoice and exult, and let us together praise the Father, the Son, and the Spirit.

And then he will rise, and having kissed Mary, will sit in his place as before, and the instruments will be played softly. Then Ecclesia will rise from her stool, and standing looking at Mary will sing in a loud voice saying:

Let the heavens rejoice and the earth exult![32] Behold our Redemption approaches, behold the Congregation of the sons of God approaches!

And pointing to herself with her right hand holding the gold ball she will say:

Behold the New Mother with breasts full not of law but grace, not fear but love, not servitude but liberty, because behold this Virgin (*pointing to Mary*) who will conceive and bear a son who will make his people safe from their sins.[33] Glory be to the Father and to the Son and to the Holy Ghost; as it was in the beginning, is now, and ever shall be, world without end.

And all the angels will respond, "Amen." And Ecclesia will stay in her place sitting on her stool as before. And after some playing Synagoga will rise to her feet in her place, with her face bowed to the left side, turn in all directions as if sad, and as if weeping will sing saying:

Who will give a fountain of tears to my eyes, that I might weep my miserable desolation.[34] Behold her (*pointing to Mary*), through whom that truth will be verified: when the Holy of Holies will come, our anointing will cease.[35]

[32] Based upon Isaias 49:13 and Psalm 96:11.
[33] Based upon Isaias 7:14 and Matthew 1:21.
[34] See Jeremias 9:1.
[35] This prophecy is found in a Pseudo-Augustinian sermon on the birth of Christ (printed in Young, *Drama of the Medieval Church*, 2:126–127), which sermon became in the Middle Ages the basis for the *Ordo Prophetarum*, one of the standard plays of the mystery cycles. This prophecy, attributed to Daniel, is apparently a misreading of Daniel 9:24, which says that the anointing of a holy of holies will signal the beginning of a reign of everlasting justice. See Young's discussion of this text in *Drama*, 2:304–305.

Then suddenly Gabriel and Raphael will come and as if with indignation expel Synagoga from the platform by the west stairs; and Synagoga while descending will throw the banner and tablet to the right and to the left in the temple[36] off the platform, and so standing straight will flee crying and murmuring outside the church, nor will she appear again. And Gabriel and Raphael will not descend from the platform but will return to their places; and the instruments will be played for a little, until the people have stopped laughing at the expulsion of Synagoga. While the instruments are still being played, Michael will ascend to the platform and lead behind him Lucifer as if unwilling to come and howling, and after Michael bows to Mary, he will station himself where the angels sang their songs, and Lucifer will be next to Michael, but when he crosses in front of Mary, he will pretend to be fearful and trembling, and he will try to hide his face. And Michael will pull him as if with great force to the place mentioned above, that is, where the angels said their verses. Then Michael, his face turned toward Mary, holding his shining sword on high and in his left hand holding Lucifer's chain, will say in a loud voice, genuflecting:

Hail, Most High Lady, whom heaven, earth, the sea, the abyss, and all creatures obey, command and I shall obey you.

And pointing to Lucifer with the point of his sword, he will say:

Behold the rebel against God, the scandal of the angels, and the enemy of human nature. But you have received from God the power to trample on, repulse, and torture him on behalf of almighty God. He will suffer your condemnation, he will be led by your will, and he will be chained under your feet.

And then Michael will put Lucifer, still bound and howling, under Mary's feet, who will pound on him with her feet and then push him from her;[37] and immediately he will be thrown off the platform by the west stairs on to the floor by Michael, Gabriel, and Raphael, nor will he appear further in the play, and the instruments will begin

[36] This stage direction assumes that the dramatic action of the Presentation Play has indeed taken place "in the temple," from which, at this point, Synagoga, representing the Old Law, is expelled.

[37] Mary's kicking of Lucifer is both a confirmation of the prophecy (Genesis 3:15) that the woman shall bruise the head of the serpent (who caused her fall), and of God's ability to make his enemies his footstool (Psalm 110:1; Matthew 22:44; 1 Corinthians 13:25).

24

playing. Michael will then take the place where Synagoga had been, continuously looking towards Mary. After a short interval Ecclesia will rise from her place, and bow before Mary, and descend from the platform to stand with the angels in her position, and after Ecclesia the two musicians will go down playing their instruments, and immediately after them the two virgins will descend carrying in their hands their candles. And Mary with her candle will descend immediately after them, between Gabriel and Raphael, although a little ahead of them without an interval, to the company of the angels in their places previously set out. Then at once Joachim and Anna will go down, and lastly Michael as if regulating the whole procession, which will go through the choir to the high altar, where the bishop is waiting with his deacon and subdeacon, dressed in a chasuble for the celebration of the Mass, the deacon and subdeacon on his right and left at the altar, all turning their faces to Mary as she approaches. When Michael comes down from the platform with Mary and her company, the space between the two rows of spears will be clear for the march toward the altar, and immediately two of the angels in a loud voice will begin:

Come, Creator, Spirit,[38]

and all the angels will respond, " Visit the minds of your own," the whole verse; and the verse finished, the two angels will begin again, " You who are called Paraclete," and so on. And the others will respond as before. The whole hymn may be completed if the procession goes toward the altar at a very slow pace. When Mary finds herself before the altar, the angels will split up in front of the altar to the right and left of Mary, Mary remaining on the step of the altar before the bishop between Joachim and Anna, Gabriel and Raphael remaining a little in back of Mary with their staves as if guarding her, and the two virgins to the right and left. Joachim and Anna will stand erect; Ecclesia will place herself at the right corner of the altar, turning her face to Mary or to the people. And Michael will face the same way in the left corner of the altar. When the hymn is over, the two singing angels will begin:

Send forth your spirit and they will be created,

and the others will respond:

[38] For the text and translation of the popular hymn *Veni creator spiritus*, see Appendix II.

And you shall renew the face of the earth.[39]

Then the bishop will say in a loud voice:

> God, who instructs the hearts of the faithful with the light of the Holy Spirit, give us to know rightly by the same Spirit, and always to rejoice in its consolation.

And after the "Come, Creator, Spirit" has begun, the instruments will no longer be played. And one thing to be noted is, that when Mary with her companions has gotten in front of the altar and the angels have split up, as is described above, those able-bodied men who carry the spears in two rows will form in front of the altar a large enclosure of their spears, in which enclosure Mary and her companions will be without pressure, nor will the sergeants at arms permit any person to come in save of the company, so that the mystery of the Presentation of Mary will be able to be seen by all without impediment.

Now all those things up to the Presentation of the Blessed Mary in the temple have been lucidly presented as they are figured in gestures, words, actions, and representations from her ascent of the stairs to her Presentation; and it should be apparent how much virtue there is in the *laudes* for her and the songs interspersed here and there concerning both catholic fundamentals and the joy of our redemption and restoration. Now to the Presentation of Mary itself, which Presentation is celebrated not without cause by the faithful today in the Church, with exultation to those devoted to the Mother of God, and with happiness among the angels. Anna standing with the bread raised in her left hand and with her right holding the left arm of Mary says in a loud voice:

> Accept, Lord, our Fruit ordained through you from eternity, blessed by you, announced through your angel, miraculously conceived, gloriously born, governed by you, and chosen by you for His Habitation.

Then Joachim standing with the wine raised in his right hand and with his left hand holding the right arm of Mary which is holding up the candle, also says in a loud voice:

> Blessed be the Lord God of Israel, because he has visited us with offspring, and he has prepared the redemption of his people.

[39] Psalm 103:30, used as a response in the Mass.

Accept, Lord, our votive offering, the Fruit of our sterility, because you have consoled us in our old age as you ordered the salvation of Jacob.[40] Come quickly, and descend to her, that your prophets may be found trustworthy, and human kind be redeemed from Babylonian servitude through her.

Which having said, Joachim and Anna will pray with heads slightly bowed toward the ground. And at once they will arise, and lead Mary, holding the candle and dove, before the bishop, and they will present her to him genuflecting. Then the bishop will say in a loud voice, in the person of God the Father:

Come my Beloved, come my Dove, because there is no spot on you. Come from Lebanon, my Chosen from eternity, that I might accept you as Bride for my beloved Son.[41]

And then the bishop will receive her in his arms, turning to the right and the left, and have her kiss the altar, and put her down on the ground. Joachim and Anna will offer the bread and wine on the altar, kissing it and leaving Mary in front of the altar with the two virgins who will also kiss the altar, and they will go down with the angels. Then Gabriel and Raphael will lead Mary between them to the platform built between the altar and the choir on the north side as declared above. And the two virgins also will climb on to the platform with Mary, on which little platform no one will remain except Mary with the two virgins, Gabriel and Raphael being stationed at the foot of the platform behind Mary with their staves held up as if to guard her. In front of Mary's little stool, on which she will rest while hearing Mass, will be three candlesticks, in which the candles of Mary and the virgins will be placed, and on the stool will be a certain pretty little book, whose pages Mary will turn as if saying her hours, and at such a time she will sit on the large cushion, and the virgins near her on the rug. During the Gospel Mary and the virgins will rise and hold their candles in their hands, and throughout the Mass Mary will conduct herself with maturity and devotion, Gabriel and Raphael giving her instructions. When the Mass is about

[40] Apparently a reference to Rachel's late childbearing, which produced Joseph and Benjamin to console Jacob's old age. The manuscript reads *salutos*, but this reading may be for *solutos*, in which case the passage would read, ". . . as you ordered the *release* of Jacob." See Young's note, *Drama*, 2:240.
[41] Based upon Canticles 4:7–8.

27

to begin, Mary will let her dove fly away. And let it be noted that when Mary is placed on the little platform, Joachim, Anna, Ecclesia, Michael, the nine angels, and the musicians playing, each one in his order with the angels first, then Ecclesia, the musicians, Joachim and Anna, and Michael, will retire back again in procession, first bowing their heads toward the bishop and the altar, and afterwards deeply before Mary, with the instruments playing, and will go to the place where they had readied themselves,[42] and take off their costumes and ornaments, all of which ornaments will be carefully stored away for performances in future years.

The above having gone away from before the bishop and Mary, the bishop will begin the *Confiteor* and the singers of the choir will begin the *Gaudeamus* of the office of the Presentation of Mary, Mary herself remaining on the platform until the end of the Mass, her face turned toward the south side, and the virgins and two angels will seem as if continually looking toward Mary. And if it seems that a brief sermon concerning the feast could be made in the Mass, and that the time will allow it, let it be done. But because the mystery will be long and devout, it is left to the judgment of the director, with the provision that, however, either in the Mass or after the meal there will by no means be lacking a sermon or preaching to the Queen of heaven, as such a feast requires.

Then when the Mass is over, Mary will come down from the platform to her angels and the virgins, and kissing the altar, will offer her candles, and the virgins likewise. And at once the musicians, who had recessed, will come back, and with them preceding and playing, Mary, between Gabriel and Raphael, with the virgins behind, in the company of a multitude of noble ladies and particularly of boys and girls of both sexes, will be carried to the house where she will eat, either by some men of large stature or riding on a palfrey; and with the angels also on two horses, Mary between them, making a brief circuit of the town if the weather is nice. During the meal also Mary, still in her costume, will be placed in the highest place in a regal seat, in the company of the virgins at the table, Gabriel and Raphael serving them with diligent solicitude and profound reverence to the end of the meal.

And whoever will be able to serve the most sweet Virgin Mary

---

[42] This direction applies to all the players except the musicians, who will return at the end of the Mass to accompany Mary and the virgins and angels from the church.

more fervently and ardently, and will be capable of repeating and enunciating her *laudes*, considering them most worthy, let him, I pray, extend his hand to me in an oath, for truly he will not make his effort in vain. And it will be noted that the songs of the *laudes* of the Virgin written above, which will be sung in a loud voice by the angels and other persons as outlined above, are most devout and will to the greatest extent raise tears of devotion in the faithful who know Latin; but since the common people do not know Latin, if it seems expedient and if our most sweet Mary will inspire it in the hearts of her devout through grace, the aforesaid songs may be translated into vernacular compositions and can thus be recited in the vernacular. This I leave to be done or not done at the discretion of the devotees of the spotless Virgin who read piously the present representation. In addition, concerning this feast of the Presentation of the Blessed Virgin Mary in the Temple brought newly shining from the Eastern to the Western regions: the manner in which the Blessed Virgin made known her wish that her feast be celebrated in these regions, the form in which it was to be celebrated in Italy and afterwards in the Roman Curia, and by whom and with how much virtue and devotion her feast was established; all these things will appear more clearly to the reader of the letter concerning the Presentation of Mary in the Temple and its introduction to the Western regions. The letter[43] should be placed before the introduction to the Office of the Presentation; and I humbly pray that anyone devoted to Mary who reads the letter, office, and present representation, to the extent of his new devotion to the Virgin, will deign to intercede for my miserable soul before the Empress of the Empyrean Heaven herself, the Anchor of my hope.

AMEN

[43] This obviously refers to the Letter printed below, pp. 51–58, which in the manuscript does precede—though not immediately—the office of the feast.

The Latin Text

Quibusdam deuotis personis Matris illius qui dat sapientiam sapientibus et scientiam intelligentibus disciplinam, qui reuelat profunda et abscondita et nouit in tenebris constituta, cum quo lux est reuelans misteria que ventura sunt, a quo omne donum optimum et perfectum descendit, reuelare placuit ut xxj^a die Nouembris pro commmemoratione diei illius quo eius eterni uerbi Mater per carnales parentes in templo Domini extitit presentata, vt sibi cui seruire regnare est in perpetuum assisteret, immaculata secundum eorum vota aliquam ordinauerunt solempnitatem cum representationibus quibusdam deuotissimis verbis nouisque actibus et signis ornatis ex quibus omnibus in Christo credentibus declararent quod per hanc humillime Virginis presentacionem in templo omnia catholica fundamenta incepta sunt, ex quibus etiam a carne mens agrauata tamquam per visiblia signa et opera secundum apostoli doctrinam ad cognitionem inuisibilium visibiliumque misteriorum Dei peruenire valerent, vt in sequentibus lucide declaratur.

Et primo de xxij. personis et nominibus ipsarum pro representatione fienda.

Secundo de indumentis ipsarum et ornamentis diuersis.

Tercio qualiter pro representationibus omnibus locus ordinetur.

Quarto de processione fienda et ordine ipsius.

Quinto de representatione fienda et laudibus Marie.

Sexto de Presentatione Marie solempni Missa celebranda et breui sermone.

Primo namque erit quedam virgo iuuencula et pulcherrima circiter trium aut iiij^or annorum, que representabit Mariam, et cum ea alic due Virgines pulcherrime eiusdem etatis. Deinde erunt Ioachim et Anna; ceterum erunt duo angeli, Gabriel et Raphael. Deinde erunt nouem Angeli representantes nouem ordines angelorum. Postea erit quedam mulier pulcherrima etatis circiter xx. annorum, que vocabitur Ecclesia, et representabit ecclesiam. Deinde erit quedam mulier prouecte etatis, que vocabitur Synagoga, et representabit legem Moysi et Vetus Testamentum. Ceterum erunt duo iuuenes cum instrumentis pulsantes. Deinde erit Michael archangelus et Lucifer. Vltimo erit episcopus cum dyacono et subdiacono.

Dicto de nominibus personarum pro representatione fienda, dicendum est de indumentis et ornamentis ipsarum.

Maria vero tunicam habebet indutam albissimam de cendato, sine aliquo artificio superfluo, cum plicatura parua eiusdem tunice exterius apparente circa inferiorem partem tunice in circulo, et tunica lata erit ubique exceptis manicis, que erunt adiacentes, nec super tunicam se cinget. Postea habebit quendam mantellum etiam albissimum de cendato aut panno serico, apertum ante in longitudinem corporis cum cordula de frizello aureo in firmatione mantelli ante pectus secundum formam mantelli sponsarum, et circa collare tunice et aperturam mantelli in longitudine apponetur paruus frizellus aureus, et in circulo mantelli inferius erit etiam plicatura apparens exterius ipsius mantelli. Capud autem Marie nudum erit, et capilli extensi retro super humeros; habebit autem super capud quemdam circulum aureum de argento deaurato in latitudine modici digiti cum diademate rationabilis latitudinis de argento deaurato subtili firmato in circulo in posteriori parte capitis. Hoc erit ornamentum capitis Marie, nec anulos nec zonam nec aliquid aliud super se habebit nisi album et aureum, puritatem et virginitatem Marie demonstrans et caritatis claritatem ipsius.

Due autem Virgines associantes Mariam: vna induetur de cerico seu cendato viridi, figurante humilitatem Marie, et alia de colore blauio seu celestino, fidem et spem Marie figurante; nam secundum apostolum conuersatio nostra, sed pocius Marie, in celis est. Iste due Virgines mantellum non portabunt sicut Maria, sed tunicas latas habebunt cum plicatura inferiori, ut supra dictum est; nec etiam ornentur super tunicas. Super capud vero nudum portabunt vnum circulum de argento sine diademate in latitudine prius declarata; et capilli extensi retro, ut supra de Maria.

Ioachim vero, pater Marie, induetur alba sacerdotis desuper cinctus velud sacerdos cum stola ad collum, et ante pectus in cruce procedente ut sacerdos, et desuper quodam pluuiali antiquo non fracto, et in capite habebit quoddam velum subtile et aliquantulum longum et, si inuenietur, aliqualiter laboratum, cum quo inuoluet capud et collum et duas extremitates veli qualibet longitudine duarum palmarum et modicum plus proiciet super humeros super pluuiale a dextris et a sinistris; habebit ante prolixam amplam et albam barbam procedentem super pectus, et tenebit in manu extra pluuiale vnum vas mediocre vitreum plenum vino rubeo.

Anna vero induetur de lino albo, tam in corpore quam in capite ad modun antique honeste matrone, et portabit in manu vnum pannum rotundum albissimum et satis magnum.

Duo autem angeli induti erunt, Gabriel et Raphael, cum amictibus albis cincti desuper cum stola ad collum et in cruce ante pectus. Super capud uero portabunt quasdam barretas adiacentes in capite super aures, et in circulo capitis desuper habebunt formam triangularem aut quadrangularum non nimis latas, cum duabus fanis retro velud in mitra episcopi. Et erunt iste barrete de cendato albo seu panno sericeo aut de papiro seu de pergamento cum quodam frizello in circulo barreti de pictura aliqua et floribus seminatis picture super barretam, et qui voluerit, poterit ponere in circulo barretarum paruas fringias de cerico diuersi coloris. Habebunt etiam duo angeli quilibet duas alas, et portabunt in manu dextra quilibet vnam virgam rubeam.

Nouem Angeli induentur sicut Gabriel et Raphael, excepto quod tres qui representabunt superiorem ordinem angelorum, scilicet cherubim et cetera, habebunt barretas suas rubeas de pictura, ut dictum; tres vero secundi ordinis angelorum habebunt barretas blauias seu celestini coloris; et tres tercij ordinis angelorum, albas barretas. Habebunt omnes nouem lilium super quandam virgam subtilem viridis coloris, et lilium primi ordinis deauratum erit, et lilium secundi ordinis celestini coloris, et tertium argentei coloris.

Ecclesia vero erit quidem pulcerrimus iuuenis circa xx. annos sine barba, et induetur totum de auro in habitu diaconi, capillis pulcerrimis mulieris extensis super humeros; et super capud portabit quandam coronam auream cum lilijs et lapidibus preciosis. Contra pectus vero erit firmatus cum cordula quidam calix argenteus et deauratus sine patena, qui calix significabit Nouum Testamentum; et in manu sinistra portabit quandam crucem longam latitudine corporis, et capitis cuius crucis virga rubea erit latitudine pollicis magni, et crux tota deaurata erit sine aliquo artificio. In manu vero dextra portabit quoddam pomum rotundum totum deauratum significans vniuersalem dominationem ecclesie.

Synagoga vero induetur ad modum antique vetule cum tunica talari inueterata alicuius panni simplicis coloris, et mantello nigro et rupto. Capud vero ad modum vetule ornatum de aliquo velo obscuri coloris, et coram oculis et facie habebit velum nigrum, per quod tamen possit videre. In manu vero sinistra portabit quoddam vexillum rubeum cuius hasta nigra fracta apparebit, vexillo inclinato super humeros suos. In quo quidem vexillo rubeo scribentur litere de auro: S. P. Q. R., que sunt arma Romanorum. Et in manu dextera portabit duas tabulas lapideas inclinatas versus terram, in quibus lapideis erunt scripte litere quasi litere Hebreorum significantes legem Moysi et Vetus Testamentum.

Duo Iuuenes qui pulsabunt instrumenta dulcia induti erunt sicut Angeli, excepto quod non portabunt stolas neque alas, sed bene barretas viridis coloris.

Deinde erit Michael archangelus, qui armatus erit armis pulcerrimis de pede usque ad capud, et super galeam seu bachinetum seu barbutam habebit quandam coronam deauratam in signum militis victoriosi et in signum Christi triumphantis. In manu autem dextra tenebit Michael gladium nudum fulgentem et erectum versus celum; et in sinistra manu tenebit quandam cathenam ferream, cum qua Lucifer in collo ligatus retro sequetur Michaelem.

Lucifer autem ornetur tali ornamento sicut eidem decet turpissimo et abhominabili, cum cornubus, dentibus et facie horribili. Et cum manu dextra tenebit Lucifer quendam trocum seu vncum ferreum portando super humerum; et cum sinistra manu tenebit cathenam, quasi rebellare vellet Michaeli.

Qualiter pro representatione fienda locus ordinetur.

In ecclesia namque inter portam magnam occidentalem et portam chori canonicorum seu fratrum in medio ecclesie, aliquantulum tamen magis prope portam chori quam prope portam occidentalem, vt ab omnibus partibus ecclesie lucidius videri possit, construetur quoddam edificium de lignis seu stacio in altitudine vj. pedum desuper, vero erit tabulatum ad modum solarij, quod quidem solarium in transuerso ecclesie, scilicet de aspectu partis septentrionalis ad partem australem habebit x. pedes in longitudine, et de aspectu partis orientalis ad occidentalem solarium habebit in latitudine viij. pedes; et contra medium solarij versus portam occidentalem erunt gradus tot quot esse poterunt de pauimento ecclesie usque ad solarium, et similiter erunt similes gradus in opposito porte chori, ad descendendum de solario, ita quod quilibet gradus in se longitudinem circiter trium pedum, vt minus occupet solarium quam fieri poterit, et isti gradus ab utraque parte clausi erunt cum tabulis seu lignis ita quod nemo ascendere valeat nisi cum ordine ad representationem faciendam. Desuper vero solarium in via inter vtrosque gradus via plana erit; sed ad partem septentrionalem erit quoddam scampnum ad sedendum protensum supra solarium de parte occidentali ad partem orientalem, et istud scampnum ita longum erit ut Ioachim et Anna in capitibus scampni et Maria in medio sedere valeant, ita tamen quod sedes Marie tantum eleuetur, ut, sedentibus ipsis tribus, capud Marie sedentis in medio in equalitate altitudinis cum patre et matre inueniatur. Et inter scampnum et extremitatem solarij versus partem septentrionalem dimittetur spacium pro Gabriele et Raphaele, qui ibidem stabunt retro Mariam in pedibus. Ad partem autem australem super solarium vltra viam graduum erunt due sedes ita alte sicut scampnum predictum, super quibus sedebunt Ioachim et Anna, quarum sedium vna erit posita ad partem orientalem solarij et alia ad partem occidentalem, super quibus sedebunt Ecclesia et Synagoga respicientes Mariam, ita quod ascendendo gradus in solarium ascendens ire possit libere inter Ecclesiam et Synagogam ad extremitatem partem solarij uersus partem australem. In quatuor vero cornibus solarij stabunt in pedibus ad cornua septentrionalia Gabriel et Raphael, et ad cornua partis australis stabunt in pedibus duo iuuenes pulsatores. Solarium vero in circuitu suo munietur quodam ligno subtili altitudinis a solario duorum pedum per modum appodiationis, ut dictum solarium magis aptum appareat ad representationem fiendam, et ne illi qui super solario erunt a solario leuiter cadere possint. Istud solarium, scampnum et sedes cooperientur de tapetis. Fiat igitur edificium seu solarium de lignis fortissimis et bene ligatis ne propter pressuram populi astantis aliquomodo cadere valeat.

Insuper inter sedes canonicorum seu fratrum et altare maius ad partem septentrionalem contra parietem seu pilare in loco eminenti construetur aliud solarium de lignis magnis, tamen paruum, videlicet in altitudine vij. uel viij. pedum. Solarium namque desuper erit quadratum sex pedum, in qualibet quadratura et in circulo etiam munietur quodam ligno subtili vnius pedis altitudinis a solario. Et cooperietur solarium de tapetis, et super tapetum quasi in medio solarij ponetur paruum scabellum coopertum de aliquo panno pulcro serico cum cussino paruo serico ad apodiandam Mariam audiendo Missam. Et recte in medio solarij super tapetum ponetur cussinus maior de serico ad sedendum Mariam, et scabellum predictum immediate ante Mariam.

Ordinabitur etiam de aliquo loco prope ecclesiam, sicut de quadam camera per terram sufficienti ad recipiendum omnes personas pro representatione ordinandas seu induendas, qui locus forte poterit esse capitulum fratrum, clausum tamen ante cum cortinis de aliqua domo prope ecclesiam ad hoc sufficienti, in qua Maria nostra dulcissima cum societate sua parabitur et parata et ornata ut supra declaratum est expectabit processionem.

De processione fienda et ordine ipsius.

Episcopus namque seu archiepiscopus Missam celebraturus indutus pontificalibus cum baculo pastorali, diacono et subdiacono precedentibus cum omni clero, sacerdotibus indutis pluuialibus seu reliquijs de altari maiori, incipiet processionem cantando alta voce *Salue Regina*, et ibit processio recta via versus locum vbi Maria erit, semper cantando. Et cum tota processio transierit locum seu capitulum, episcopo immediate transacto, aperientur cortine seu porta. Et primo exibit vnus de ordine Angelorum cum virga alba in manu sua dextra, quasi ad ostendendum et parandum viam, et sequetur iste Angelus immediate episcopum quasi ad duos passus prope eum, ita tamen quod nulla persona se interponat inter episcopum et Angelum; Angelus autem sequendo episcopum proportionaliter cum virga sua a dextris et a sinistris parabit viam. Et post Angelum sequentur alij octo Angeli, vnus post alterum gradiendo secundum ordinem suum, et ierarchiam cherubim et cheraphim retrogradientibus quilibet portando in manu sua sinistra lilium supra declaratum. Post nouem Angelos immediate sequetur Synagoga, capite dimisso, et portando vexillum suum et tabulas lapideas, ut supra declaratum est. Et post Synagogam sequetur Ecclesia formosa cum sua cruce, calice in pectore et pomo aureo in manu dextra. Post Ecclesiam immediate sequentur duo iuuenes Pulsatores gradientes insimul et pulsantes instrumenta. Post Pulsatores sequentur duo Virgines gradientes insimul, et illa que induta erit colore viridi portabit in manu dextra vnam candelam tercie partis libre viridis coloris, et alia Virgo similem candelam celestini coloris.

Post duas Virgines immediate sequetur nostra dulcissima Maria portando in manu sua dextra similem candelam in pondere albissimam tamen, et in manu sua sinistra portabit quandam columbam

35

albissimam ad pectus suum; et ad latus Marie dextrum gradietur Gabriel cum virga sua rubea eleuata; et ad latus sinistrum Marie simili modo Raphael gradiens in equalitate cum Maria reuerenter, nec nimis approprinquantes ad personam Marie, sed eam semper rescipientes.

Post Mariam, Gabrielem et Raphaelem gradientur simul Ioachim et Anna respicientes continue Mariam, et portantes panem et vinum, ut supra declaratum est. Et post ipsos veniet Michael archangelus armatus cum gladio fulgenti et erecto in manu dextra, et cum sinistra per cathenam vnius passus ducendo trahet Luciferum cachinnantem et aliquando vlulantem, et quasi inuitum incendentem.

Maria autem exeunte de capitulo seu loco ubi ipsa processiones exspectabat, subito vnus de Angelis ponet se inter duos Pulsatores eundo processionaliter et alta voce inchoabit quandam cantilenam per modum rondelli instrumentis pulsantibus de Beatissima Virgine, et hec in vulgari ad excitandum populum ad deuotionem. Et omnes Angeli cum Ecclesia, Gabrieli et Raphaeli et Pulsatoribus respondebunt. Clerus vero qui ante cantabat *Salue Regina,* quando audiet Angelum canentem, tacebit, et omnes tacebunt exceptis Angelis qui continue dictum rondellum cantabunt, vno inchoante et alijs respondentibus processionaliter eundo usque ad solarium in medio ecclesie constructum.

Et post Michaelem et Luciferum gradientur nobiles et persone autentice vulgares, et postea populus vtriusque sexus. Ibit autem processio per claustrum usque ad portam que ducit ad plateam que est ante valuas magnas ecclesie occidentales. In qua quidem platea processio faciet quendam circulum circuiendo plateam et reuertendo ad magnam portam ecclesie gradiendo et cantando ut supra usque ad solarium predictum. Et notandum est quod quelibet persona de clero eundo processionaliter portabit vnam candelam accensam in manu, et si nobiles persone autentice et populus portare uoluerint candelas in processione illius noui luminis ex vtero postea illuminantis vniuersum orbem, ab ipso lumine non dubito premiabitur. Cum autem Maria de capitulo cum societate sua exibit, erunt ordinati certi homines iuuenes et robusti qui hastas lancearum cum fune in transuerso inuicem ligatas in manibus tenebunt in longitudine ab episcopo usque ad Luciferum inclusiue, et hoc duplici ordine gradiendo processionaliter, vt videlicit Maria cum sua societate adornata eundo inter hastas a pressura populi non molestetur et habeat viam expeditam; ita tamen quod homines tenentes hastas in manibus in transuerso extra hastas versus populum ab utraque parte gradientur sustinendo populum cum hastis ne aliquis inter duos ordines hastarum intrare valeat nisi Maria et societas sua, exceptis duobus tribus aut quatuor seruientibus aut clientibus iusticie qui inter hastas esse poterunt ad sedandum pressuram populi, ne Maria et societas sua a populo opprimi valeant.

Intrante autem processione in ecclesiam, Episcopus cum clero suo transiet iuxta solarium et ibit ad altare maius, ibique in cathedra sua expectabit cum clero representationem fiendam super solarium, et postea Presentationem Marie ad ipsum Episcopum fiendam. Et Maria cum societate sua inter hastas coram solario constructo firmiter stabit inter solarium et magnam portam ecclesie occidentalem, Angelis semper cantantibus tantum quod Episcopus ad cathedram suam peruenire valeat et totus populus in ecclesiam intrauerit. Et nota quod processio valde mane circa solis ortum incipi debeat, quia misterium representationis prolixum est et deuotissimum, et dies tunc breues sunt.

De Representatione fienda et Laudibus Marie.

Representatio talis est. Gabriel et Raphael cum Maria, Ioachim et Anna et duobus Pulsatoribus pulsantibus et preeuntibus ad pedem graduum solarij properabunt, alijs Angelis, Ecclesia, Synagoga, Michaele et Lucifero in ordine suo firmiter stantibus et exspectantibus. Per seruientes autem armorum seu clientes ascensus graduum solarij solicite custodiatur, ne aliqui ascendere presumant nisi ad representationem fiendam ordinati. Tunc Gabriel primus in solarium ascendet, et cum virga sua voluendo se ad omnem plagam nutu non verbo omnibus silencium inponet cum virga. Et subito Maria sola sine adiutorio aliquo per gradus in solarium hylari facie ascendet, et si non poterit portare candelam suam ascendendo, Raphael eam candelam portabit, et Maria columbam suam coram pectore suo ascendendo portabit, instrumentis pulsantibus. Et quando Maria erit super solarium erecta facie uersus altare maius, statim Raphael ascendet et vna cum Gabriele Mariam ponent in sedem suam superius declaratam versus septentrionalem partem. Et tunc Gabriel et Raphael insimul cum profunda reuerentia adorabunt Mariam et ibunt retro ipsam, Gabriel in cornu solarij versus orientem pedibus stando Mariam semper respiciendo et virga erecta, et sic Raphael in alio cornu solarij retro Mariam virga erecta. Maria autem tenebit cum ambabus manibus columbam in gremio suo ipsam aliquando osculando et ponendo ad pectus suum. Et candela Marie ponetur per Raphaelem super vnum candelabrum coram Maria; et sic ponentur due candele duarum Virginum, quando ascense erunt, in solario super duo candelabra in equalitate candelabri Marie. Tunc ascendent due Virgines insimul tenentes candelas suas, et ponent se ad pedes Marie sedendo. Et postea duo Pulsatores ascendent et ponent se in cornubus solarij versus australem partem, quilibet in vno cornu solarij, respicientes Mariam et pulsantes. Statim post ascensionem Pulsatorum ascendent Ioachim et Anna, et capite modicum inclinato quasi reuerendo Mariam, sedebunt super scampnum superius declaratum, Maria in medio versa facie versus partem australem, Ioachim ad sinistram Marie uersus orientem, et Anna uersus dextram Marie uersus occidentem sedendo. Et statim ascendent Synagoga primo et post eam Ecclesia, et sedebunt super scabella sua prius declarata, scilicet Synagoga ad partem orientalem et Ecclesia ad partem occidentalem, respicientes Mariam et tenentes in manibus Synagoga vexillum et tabulas, et Ecclesia crucem et pomum, ut supra declaratum est. Et sic remanebit via expedita in solario inter duos gradus inter ascensum solarij occidentalem et descensum ipsius orientalem inter Mariam, Ioachim et Annam equaliter sedentes, Gabriele et Raphaele retro in cornubus solarij partis septentrionalis stantibus et pulsantibus inter Synagogam et Ecclesiam, Pulsatoribus retro in cornubus solarij partis australis stantibus et pulsantibus.

Nunc autem veniendo ad Laudes Marie primo silentio inposito per Gabrielem et Raphaelem cum virgis suis, primus Angelus qui tenebit virgam albam in manu dextra et lilium suum in manu sinistra ascendet in solarium virga erecta; et cum venerit ante Mariam, ponet virgam suam super tapetum et profunde Mariam inclinabit, et statim ponet se inter Synagogam et Ecclesiam et Pulsatores facie erecta uersus Mariam tenentibus instrumentis et omnibus de Ecclesia tenendo lilium erectum in manu sinistra et cum manu dextra uersus Mariam alta voce quasi cantando incipiet dicere:

Que est illa que ascendit per desertum sicut virgula fumi ex aromatibus mirre et thuris? Estne illa virga que egredietur de radice Iesse, et flos de radice eius ascendit et requiescit super eum spiritus Domini, spiritus sapientie et intellectus, spiritus scientie et concilij, spiritus pietatis et fortitudinis, et spiritus timoris Domini?

Quo dicto, pulsabuntur instrumenta, et dictus Angelus veniet coram Maria, et inclinando se coram ea accipiet virgam suam et descendet de solario per gradus partis orientalis, et tenebit se inter gradus et hostium chori, ubi erunt iuuenes homines robusti tenentes hastas in transuerso duplici ordine, ut prius declaratum est, ad recipiendum et Angelos et Mariam quando descendent de solario, et ibunt per chorum ad altare maius ad presentandum Mariam Episcopo. Primo autem Angelo descendente de solario, pulsantibus instrumentis, secundus Angelus ascendet in solarium per gradus occidentales, et cum lilio suo in manu sinistra profunde Mariam inclinabit et ponet se in loco vbi fuerat Angelus inter Ecclesiam, Synagogam et pulsatores, et simili modo tenendo lilium erectum in manu sinistra, et dextram extendendo ad Mariam alta voce dicet:

Ecce appropinquat gaudium nostrum,

cum manu a dextris et a sinistris vertendo, et reducendo ad Mariam dicet:

Considerate et videte speciosam virginem, Deo placentem, claritate refulgentem, angelos letificantem, in honestate perseuerantem, et mundum decorantem. Dies immense leticie et magne exultationis omnibus creaturis, quia ecce archa Domini, vasculum diuine sapientie, et conseruatio naufragantis nature, que hodie in templo presentatur, Deo dedicatur et in perpetuum ad honorem omnipotentis Dei obligatur.

Quo dicto, instrumenta pulsentur et Angelus inclinet se coram Maria et descendat cum primo Angelo, stetque in ordine suo exspectando. Tercius autem Angelus in loco vbi supra dicet:

Virgo ascendit in templum, et angeli descendunt ad eam. Hec ancilla vocatur et domina erit; humilis dicitur et Deum humiliabit; virginitatem vouet et Deum generabit. Tu es virgo, exemplum virginum, mulier decus mulierum, domina regular dominarum, benedicta tu quia per te virgines decorabuntur, mulieres benedicentur, et omnes sancti per te premiabuntur.

Quartus Angelus dicet:

Ecce virginitas, ecce humilitas, ecce mansuetudo, ecce puritas, ecce innocentia, ecce perfecta caritas, in qua habitabit immensa bonitas, et ecce illa que fiet sponsa, mater, et templum Dei.

Et notandum est quod omnes Angeli in eodem loco dicent et cantabunt versus suos seu carmina, et in ascendendo in solarium stando cantando inclinando coram Maria, descendendo de solario et exspectando inter gradus solarij orientales et hostium chori tenebunt illum ordinem qui superius declaratus est de duobus primis Angelis. Quintus Angelus cantabit dicens:

O grande edificium in quo sustentabitur humana fragilitas, super quod edificabitur vniuersa fidelitas, a quo inchoatur perfecta virginitas, et in quo terminabitur immensa bonitas; a te, per te, et in te laudabitur summa diuinitas.

Sextus Angelus cantabit et dicet:

O admirabilis Domina in conspectu hominum, in conspectu angelorum, et in presentia Dei! Quis te digne laudabit, quis te digne invocabit, cum in mundo sis sine exemplo, et in natura sine macula, et in celo eris cum immensa gloria?

Septimus Angelus cantabit et dicet:

Aue, Domina nostra, aue reparatio humane nature, aue mediatrix diuine iusticie et in qua misericordia Dei ostendetur, quia tu mater et virgo eris, Deus et homo, fides et cor humanum. Certe mirabilis puelle ascendentis ascensio, sed mirabilior sapientia puelle operantis, sed mirabilissima destorsio Dei descendentibus, que sanctis Patris erit gaudium et omnibus Deum diligentibus, quia cum ea apud Deum semper gaudebimus per infinita seculorum secula.

Octauus Angelus dicet seu cantabit:

Aue, Maria, gratia plena, Dominus tecum; et plus tecum quam in celo, enim in te habitabit assumens de te carnem; tecum erit et cum omnibus qui tecum sunt, qui te diligunt, qui te honorant; tecum creator erit. O creatura Dominus, O ancilla sponsus, O admirabilis sponsa, nos te benedicimus, nos te laudamus, nos te adoramus per infinita seculorum secula.

Nonus Angelus e cherubin cantabit dicens:

O inestimabilis amor! O immensa dilectio! O infinita caritas!

seipsum cum manu propria ostendendo; deinde Mariam cum manu ostendendo dicet:

Ecce illa cui dabitur precium humane redemptionis, donum infinite estimationis, et premium summe perfectionis! Hec est illa Virgo, Mater Filij Dei humilis, que a Spiritu Sancto obumbrabitur, ancilla electissima vocabitur, et cum Deo Patre in eternum premiabitur.

Pulsantibus autem instrumentis, et ix. Angelis in ordine suo, secundum quem gradiebantur in processione, in terra exspectantibus, inter solarium et hostium chori, Anna mater Marie surget et stando pedibus in loco suo, instrumentis tacentibus, leuabit ambas manus suas ad celum cum pane in sinistra, et voce grossa mulieris vidue et prouecte dicet:

Audite, filij Israel, exultantes mecum, quia mirabilia Dei narrabo: Sterilis facta est mater (*seipsam ostendendo cum manu*), et genuit exultationem in Israel. Ecce potero offerre munera Domino, et non poterint me prohibere inimici mei. Dominus Deus exercituum factus est memor uerbi sui, et visitauit populum suum visitatione sua sancta.

Quo dicto et osculata Maria, sedebit in loco suo, ut prius, et instrumenta pulsabuntur modicum. Tunc Ioachim surget in pedibus stando in loco suo, et similiter leuabit manus ad celum cum vino in sinistra, et vertendo se a dextris et sinistris cum manibus annuendo grossa voce dicet:

Gaudete omnes mulieres, quia delebitur opprobrium vestrum; et vos omnes homines, quia Deus homo ex ea nascetur (*ostendendo Mariam cum manu; deinde ad Angelos uertendo se*); et vos omnes angeli, quia sedes vestre reparabuntur.

Deinde uertet se circumquaque et dicet:

Et vos omnes creature, quia par eam decorabimini.

Et cum manibus ad celum eleuatis, genuflectendo, facie ad partem australem sicut sederat, concludet dicens:

Gaudeamus ergo omnes et exultemus, et Patrem et Filium et Spiritum collaudemus.

Et tunc surget et, osculata Maria, sedebit in loco suo sicut prius, et pulsabuntur instrumenta modicum. Tunc surget Ecclesia de scabello suo, et stando in pedibus respiciendo Mariam cantabit alta voce dicens:

Letentur celi et exultet terra! Ecce appropinquat redempcio nostra, ecce appropinquat congregatio filiorum Dei!

Et ostendendo seipsam cum manu dextra tenendo pomum aureum dicet:

41

Ecce noua mater vbertate plena non legis sed gracie, non timoris sed amoris non seruitutis sed libertatis, quia ecce illa virgo (*demonstrando Mariam*) que concipiet et pariet filium, qui saluum faciet populum suum a peccatis eorum. Gloria Patri et Filio et Spiritui Sancto; sicut erat in principio, et nunc et semper, et in secula seculorum.

Et omnes angeli respondebunt *Amen*. Et remanebit Ecclesia in loco suo sedendo super scabellum suum sicut prius. Et post modicam pulsationem surget Synagoga in pedibus stando in loco suo, facie inclinata ad partem sinistram, quasi tristis vertet se circumquaque, et quasi flendo cantabit dicens:

Quis dabit fontem lacrimarum oculis meis, ut plorem miserabilem desolationem meam. Ecce illa (*ostendendo Mariam*), per quam verificabitur illa veritas: Cum venerit sanctus sanctorum, cessabit vnctio vestra.

Et tunc subito venient Gabriel et Raphael, et quasi cum indignatione expellentes Synagogam de solario per gradus occidentales; et tunc Synagoga descendendo proiciet vexillum et tabulas a dextris et a sinistris in templo extra solarium, et sic erecta fugiet plorando et murmurando extra ecclesiam, nec amplius apparebit. Et Gabriel et Raphael non descendent de solario, sed reuertentur in loco suo; et pulsabuntur instrumenta modicum, et tantum quod populus quietetur a risu propter Synagogam expulsam. Pulsando uero instrumenta, Michael ascendet solarium et ducet secum Luciferum quasi inuitum incedentem et vlulantem, et post inclinationem Michaelis ad Mariam ponet se ubi Angeli cantabunt carmina sua, et Lucifer erit iuxta Michaelem, sed cum transibit coram Maria, finget se timorosum et trementem, et dimittet se cadere in faciem suam. Et Michael eum quasi vi trahet ad locum prius dictum, scilicet vbi Angeli dixerunt versus suos. Tunc Michael, facie versa ad Mariam, in altum tenendo gladium fulgentem et in sinistra tenendo cathenam Luciferi genuflectentis alta voce dicet:

Aue, altissima Domina, cui celi, terra, mare, abyssi et omnes creature obediunt, precipe et ego obediam tibi.

Et cum puncto gladij ostendendo Luciferum dicet:

Ecce rebellator Dei, scandalum angelorum, et inimicus humane nature. Tu enim a Deo accepisti potestatem conculcandi, repellendi et cruciandi eum ex parte omnipotentis Dei. Tue damnationi supponitur, tue uoluntati traditur, et sub pedibus tuis vinculatur.

Et tunc Michael Luciferum sic ligatum et ululantem sub pedibus Marie ponet, que ipsum cum pedibus verberabit, ipsumque a se expellet; et statim per Michaelem, Gabrielem et Raphaelem de solario per gradus occidentales proiciatur in terram, nec amplius in festo appareat, et pulsabuntur instrumenta. Et Michael ponet se ubi erat Synagoga, respiciendo semper Mariam. Post modicum autem interuallum surget Ecclesia de loco suo, et inclinabit se coram Maria, et descendet de solario cum Angelis stando in ordine suo, et post Ecclesiam descendent duo Pulsatores pulsantes instrumenta sua, et immediate post ipsos descendent due Virgines portantes in manibus candelas suas. Et Maria cum candela sua in manu statim post eas, in medio Gabrielis et Raphaelis, modicum tamen ante ipsos sine interuallo descendet de solario in societate Angelorum in ordine suo prius declarato. Et postea immediate descendent Ioachim et Anna, et ultimo Michael quasi regens processionem, eundo per chorum ad altare maius, vbi Episcopus exspectat indutus casula pro Missa celebranda cum dyacono suo et subdyacono, vnum a dextris et alium, a sinistris erecti apodiantes se ad altare, versa facie ad Mariam venientem. Cum autem Michael descenderit de solario cum Maria et societate sua, inter duos ordines hastarum erit parata ad gradiendum versus altare, subito duo de Angelis alta voce incipient:

Veni creator spiritus.

Et omnes Angeli respondebunt *Mentes tuorum uisita*, totum versum; et finito versu, duo Angeli iterum incipient *Qui paraclitus*, et cetera. Et alij respondebunt sicut prius. Et eundo ad altare lento gradu complebitur totus hymnus. Quando vero Maria inueniet se coram altari, Angeli coram altari diuident se a dextris et sinistris Marie, Maria remanente in gradu altaris coram Episcopo inter Ioachim et Annam, Gabriele et Raphaele in medio retro Mariam remanentibus cum virgis suis quasi custodiendo Mariam, et due Virgines a dextris et sinistris. Ioachim et Anna erecti stabunt; Ecclesia autem ponet se ad dextrum cornu altaris, versa facie ad Mariam uel ad populum. Et sic faciet Michael in cornu sinistro altaris. Hymno completo, duo Angeli cantatores incipient:

Emitte spiritum tuum et creabuntur.

Et alij respondebunt:

Et renouabis faciem terre.

Tunc Episcopus alta voce dicet:

Deus, qui corda fidelium sancti Spiritus illustratione docuisti, da nobis in eodem Spiritu recta sapere, et de ejus semper consolatione gaudere.

Et postquam *Veni creator* incipietur, instrumenta amplius non pulsabunt. Vnum notandum est, quod quando Maria cum societate sua peruenerit coram altari et Angeli diuident se, ut dictum est, illi iuuenes robusti qui portabunt hastas duplici ordine coram altar facient vnum magnum quadrangulum de hastis suis in quo quadrangulo Maria et societas sua sine pressura erunt, nec permittent seruientes armorum quod aliqua persona intret nisi sit de societate Marie, vt videlicet misterium Presentationis Marie ab omnibus videri possit sine inpedimento.

Nunc autem ad Presentationem Beate Marie in Templo sciendum est quod omnia supra figurata in signis, dictis, factis et representationibus satis lucide declarant ascensionem graduum Marie Presentationemque eius; et quante uirtutis sit apparet in Laudibus ipsius et carminibus sepe replicatis et fundamentum catholicum et iocundum nostre redemptionis et reparationis. Nunc vero ad Presentationem Marie que Presentatio letantibus angelicis et Matris Dei deuotis exultantibus hodie in ecclesia Dei non immerito a fidelibus celebratur. Anna vero erecta cum pane eleuato in manu sinistra et cum dextra brachium sinistrum Marie tenendo alta voce dicet

Accipe, Domine, fructum nostrum per te ab eterno ordinatum, a te benedictum, per angelum tuum annunciatum, mirabiliter conceptum, gloriose natum, per te gubernatum, et a te in habitaculum tuum electum.

Tunc Ioachim erectus manu dextra cum vino eleuata, et cum sinistra tendo brachium dextrum Marie eleuatum cum candela, alta voce etiam dicet:

Benedictus Dominus Deus Israel, quia visitauit nos in prole, et preparauit redempcionem plebi sue. Accipe, Domine, votum nostrum, fructum sterilitatis nostre, quia consolatus es senectutem nostram, qui mandas salutos Iacob. Veni cito, et descende in eam, ut prophete tui fideles inueniantur, et genus humanum a Babilonica seruitute per eam redimatur.

Quo dicto, Ioachim et Anna capitibus in terram inclinatis modicum orabunt, Maria in pedibus remanente. Et statim surgent, et ducent Mariam tenentem candelam et columbam coram Episcopo, ipsamque

44

eidem presentabunt genibus flexis. Tunc Episcopus alta voce dicet in personam Dei Patris:

Veni amica mea, veni columba mea, quia macula non est in te. Veni de Lybano electa ab eterno, ut te accipiam sponsam dilecto filio meo.

Et tunc Episcopus eam accipiet in vlnis suis, vertendo se a dextris et sinistris, et faciet ipsam osculari altare et deponet eam in terram. Ioachim vero et Anna offerent supra altare panem et vinum osculando altare dimittentes Mariam coram altari cum duabus Virginibus, que etiam osculabuntur altare, et descendent cum Angelis. Tunc Gabriel et Raphael in medio ipsorum ducent Mariam in solarium preparatum inter altare et sedes chori ad partem septentrionalem superius declaratum. Et due Virgines etiam ascendent in solarium cum Maria, in quo solario paruo nullus remanebit nisi Maria cum duabus Virginibus, Gabriele et Raphaele retro Mariam in pedibus cum virgis suis erectis remanentibus quasi ad custodiam Marie. Ante vero scabellum paruum Marie, super quo apodiabit se audiendo Missam, erunt tria candelabra, quibus ponentur candele Marie et Virginum, et super scabellum erit quidam libellus paruulus pulcer, cuius folia Maria reuoluet quasi dicendo horas suas, et quandoque sedebit super cussinum maiorem, et Virgines prope eam super tapetum. In evvangelio surget Maria et Virgines, et tenebunt candelas in manibus, et tenebit se Maria in Missa mature et deuote, Gabriele et Raphiele eam instruentibus. Missa namque incepta, Maria columbam permittet euolare. Et notandum quod quando Maria erit super istud solarium paruum, Ioachim, Anna, Ecclesia, Michael, ix Angeli, Pulsatoribus pulsantibus, quilibet in gradu suo Angeli primi, Ecclesia, Pulsatoribus, Ioachim et Anna et Michaele retrogradientibus inclinatis capitibus coram Episcopo et altari et postea profunde coram Maria, recedent processionaliter, instrumentis pulsantibus, et ibunt ad locum ubi parauerant se, et deponent vestimenta sua et ornamenta, que omnia ornamenta sollicite custodiantur pro representatione anni futuri.

Predictis autem recedentibus a facie Episcopi et Marie, Episcopus incipiet *Confiteor*, et cantores chori incipient *Gaudeamus*, officium Presentationis, Maria in solario remanente usque ad finem Misse, facie uersa ad partem australem, et Virgines et duo Angeli quasi continue respicient Mariam. Et si videbitur quod possit fieri sermo breuis de solempnitate in Missa, et quod tempus patiatur, fiat. Sed quia misteria prolixa fuerunt et deuota, arbitrio dominorum erlinquatur, ita tamen quod aut in Missa aut post prandium tanta solempnitas Regine celi sermone seu predicatione nullo modo careat.

Missa autem finita, Maria cum Angelis suis et Virginibus de solario descendet, et osculando altare candelam suam offeret, et Virgines etiam. Et statim aderunt Pulsatores, qui recesserunt, et ipsis precedentibus et pulsantibus, Maria in medio Gabrielis et Raphaelis, Virginibus recedentibus, associata multitudine dominarum nobilium maxime puellarum et puerorum sexus vtriusque, ad domum vbi prandere velut portabitur per aliquem hominem procere stature seu equitando super palefridum; et Angeli etiam super duos equos, Maria in medio faciendo modicum circuitum per ciuitatem, si tempus fuerit serenum. In prandio autem Maria in habitu suo in loco sublimiori et cathedra regali ponatur, associata Virginibus quam plurimis in mensa, Gabriele et Raphaele vsque ad finem prandij diligenter sollicite et cum profunda reuerentia seruientibus.

Et qui dulcissimam Virginem Mariam feruentius et ardentius seruire poterit et ipsius Laudes dignissimas recensendo replicare et annunciare valuerit, mihi manum adiuratione, exoro, porrigat, quia ueraciter merito non frustrabitur. Et notandum quod carmina de Laudibus Virginis suprascripta, que per Angelos et personas alias suprascriptas alta voce cantabuntur seu proferentur, deuotissima sunt ac certe lacrimabilia pre deuotione maxime fidelibus gramaticam intelligentibus; sed quia vulgaris populus gramaticam non intelligit, si videbitur expediens et nostra Maria dulcissima in cordibus deuotorum suorum per gratiam inspirauerit, translatari poterunt sepetacta carmina in vulgari dictamine et vulgariter simili modo dictari poterunt. Istud relinquo fiendum uel non fiendum deuotis intemerate Virginis presentem representationem pie legentibus. Istam autem solempnitatem Presentationis Beate Marie Virginis in Templo nouiter choruscantem de partibus orientalibus ad partes occidentales, quomodo Beata Virgo voluit ipsam solempnitatem in dictis partibus celebrari, debere quomodo fuit celebrata in Ytalia, et postea in Curia Romana, per quem et quante virtutis et deuotionis ipsa solempnitas existat, in epistola de Presentatione Marie in Templo et nouitate eius ad partes occidentales legenti lucidius apparebit, que quidem epistola ante principium Officij Presentationis poni debet; vnde deuoto Marie legenti epistolam, officium, et presentem representationem humiliter exoro ut in tanta deuotione noua Virginis pro anima mea misera apud ipsam Inperatricem celi empyrei et anchoram spei mee intercedere dignetur. Amen.

46

A Letter and a Note
Concerning
the Presentation Play

The projects of Philippe de Mézières's later years, while he was in retirement at the Celestine Abbey in Paris, were carried out with meticulous and exhaustive care. His works were long; but he himself wrote and corrected the manuscripts of these works, and took care that they would enforce in all their details the central purposes of each work. Thus the Presentation Play is preceded in Philippe's handwritten manuscript by seven other items, as follows:

(1) A sermon on the Presentation of the Virgin Mary by Master John of Basilia, Doctor of Theology and General of the Hermit Friars of St. Augustine. This sermon was apparently preached during the Mass following a production of the Presentation Play at Avignon in 1385. See in Note below, p. 68.

(2) A letter of Philippe de Mézières, former Chancellor of Cyprus, concerning the feast of the Presentation of the Blessed Virgin Mary, printed below.

(3) The story of a miracle of Blessed Mary, in which she was invoked by two Jews who were hanging by their feet whom she released and who were subsequently baptized.

(4) The Office of the Presentation, with music.

(5) The story of the Presentation, in six readings.

(6) The Mass for the feast, with music.

(7) A Note concerning the 1385 production at Avignon, not in Philippe de Mézières's hand, printed below.

The whole manuscript is in twenty-four folios, and has written on the flyleaf statements showing that it had belonged in turn to Philippe de Mézières and to the Celestine Abbey in which he died. See Young, Drama of the Medieval Church, *2:472–473, for a full description of the manuscript and a listing, in Latin, of its contents.*

Translating the content of the Letter and the Note presents few problems, but capturing the style is most difficult. The extreme self-depreciation and the exaggerated formality of the letter would be typical of a chancellor, and are

49

even essential to his argument for the dignity and importance of this new feast; but they do not translate well into twentieth-century English. Nor is it clear, in the Latin or the English, whether the 1372, authorized, performance of the office included the Presentation Play. La Piana ("Byzantine Iconography," p. 268) believes that it did. Philippe, he says, was familiar with Eastern liturgy where essentially dramatic performances were common parts of the offices themselves. What Philippe has done, La Piana suggests, is to separate out the dramatic part of the office, in order to produce a liturgy more in accord with Western practice, while continuing to regard the play as part of the office. But it is also possible, indeed probable, that the play itself was largely Philippe's own composition, based upon what he had observed of performances in Cyprus.

The point of particular interest in the Note on the 1385 production is that, in certain details, it differs from the directions contained in the text of the play. Since Philippe had produced the 1385 performance, these divergences cannot be attributed to lack of understanding. It may well be that his formulation, however detailed, invited variations to fit momentary inspirations or local circumstances.

The Latin Text of the Letter and the Note, which follow the translations, are reproduced from Karl Young, The Drama of the Medieval Church *(Oxford: Clarendon Press, 1933), 2:473–479.*

The Letter

A letter concerning the Feast of the Presentation of the Blessed
Mary in the temple, as celebrated on the 21st of November
[1372], and its introduction into the West

To all of the faithful in the Lord, especially to the Christians of the
West, from Philippe de Mézières, lowly knight of Picardy, called
though unworthy Chancellor of the kingdom of Cyprus, and fruitless
devotee of the glorious Virgin Mary: in order to evade through
Mary the judge's sentence of high wrath, and to arrive at the life
eternal, he is compelled to cry aloud our many common sorrows, and
to recall from memory into light the evils of our nations. Indeed,
those who have been redeemed by the Lord Jesus are now saying in
tears, "Woe to us Christians! our faces are red and livid with shame;
for the inextricable evils inflicted up to now upon us Christians as
our sins have asked for them are not kept hidden today from the
sons of foreign unbelievers who surround us." And truly, the number
of pestilences, seditions, perishings, wars, treasons, and heresies which
have arisen in our times is visible to all who observe.

And because God has chastised and is continually chastising us
Christians, whether by death, or by sword, or by famine and captivity,[1] what Jeremiah prophesied and as well what Bernard wrote
to the cardinals at Ostia, Penestrina, and Tuscany may be repeated
not without relevance today: "Vice has conquered wisdom, everywhere the horn of the impious is overflowing, the zeal for justice
has been disarmed, and there is no one who, I do not say is willing,
but is able, to do good; the proud perform their iniquities anywhere,
and no one dares murmur against them; if only disregarding them

---

[1] "And if they shall say unto thee, 'Whither shall we go forth?' thou
shalt say to them, 'Thus saith the Lord: Such as are for death, to death;
and such as are for the sword, to the sword; and such as are for famine,
to famine; and such as are for captivity, to captivity'" (Jeremias 15:2).

51

were safe, or if only justice were sufficient for the defense of itself!"
Thus he said.[2]

Nor is it any wonder, dearest Fathers and Brothers, that, though
we strike the Redeemer with our prayers, he does not melt, for he is
angry with us; he turns away his face, and we are thrown into confusion. Then what is to be done in desperation? There is nothing
which will avail. Except that, in the midst of so many processes,
scourges, and perils, we may hurry surely to the port of safety, that
is, to the advocate of sinners, the Mediatrix of God and man, the
Queen of mercy and the Mother of God; we may have recourse to
the inviolate Christbearing Virgin Mary, crying out new praises,
so that she will out of pity throw open her breast to us, and, raised
to greater devotion in the enumeration of her delights through the
praise of her Presentation, will deign to intercede for our misery
before that blessed fruit of her womb, Jesus her only-begotten son,
appeasing him more than usual; we may, with her assistance and
protection, be delivered from evil, be led back to the right path,
and, with nothing to fear from the hands of our enemies, serve Him
from this time forth in sanctity and justice all our days.

Let us sing, therefore, a new song to the Queen of heaven, and let
us announce the ancient praises of Mary in her Presentation in the
Temple, newly brought shining from the Orient, to our brother
Christians on the western, northern, and southern shores of the world,
as a remedy and a joy of the spirit. All of the Catholics of Europe
and Africa, above all the devotees of the inviolate Virgin, will hear
of this most devout feast, brightening the hearts of those zealous
for the Virgin, and new in the Western Church at any rate, although
of long standing in the Eastern Church, and they will be excited to
new devotion. For from ancient times, and, as it is believed, in the
primitive church when the holy city of Jerusalem and the Holy
Land were held by Christians, and everywhere in other parts of the
Orient in which the catholic faith flourished, having been instituted
by the Holy Fathers and declared a true miracle, the feast of the
Most Blessed Evervirgin Mary—when in the third year of her life,
having ascended miraculously by herself the fifteen steps of the
temple, she was presented by her parents in the said temple—was
most devoutly and solemnly celebrated on the twenty-first day of
the month of November. And this feast is still in the kingdom of
Cyprus maintained most devoutly to the present day by the faithful

[2] Saint Bernard, *Epistola CCXXXI* (*Patrologia Latina* 182:418).

from the Orient, and the office is held entirely proper and most devout according the the use of the Court of Rome, even to the musical notation.[3]

With respect to this same feast: the above-mentioned Chancellor (although he was unworthy and unserviceable), because of his devotion to the Virgin, both anticipating with joy and feeling in his pious heart the injustice that such a feast should not be observed in the western regions where, under God's protection, the Fullness of the faith dwells, arranged the celebration of the said feast accompanied by a most devout and figurative representation performed out of reverence for the Most Blessed Evervirgin Mary and with her help several years ago in certain parts of Italy, more particularly in that splendid city of Venice, sometimes in communion with those of that city devoted to the Virgin, sometimes celebrating the feast with outsiders confirming its signs and visions and participating in it.[4] And by this means, for certain, a new and joyous devotion to the Mother of God arose in no small measure in the hearts of the faithful.

The said Chancellor, coming with many others as ambassadors of the youngest son of that most serene prince Peter, King of Jerusalem and Cyprus (formerly a Machabee, victorious and strong in arms, because of his deeds in the Orient; now a sorrowful memory to his Lord) to the feet of the most Holy Pope Gregory the Eleventh, our father in Christ and our lord in the Lord, the Highest Pontif of the Holy Roman and Universal Church; panting with all his force in hopes that the feast of the said Blessed Evervirgin Mary might be published over all the lands of the apostolic authority; with that humility of which he was capable and not that which he should have had; by means of devout orations of various sorts as well as the support and aid of many devotees of the Virgin of both sexes, trusting not in his own strength, but in the celestial ark which drew down the divine majesty even to a virgin womb, he told the said Most

---

[3] La Piana ("Byzantine Iconography," pp. 263–264) believes that the office of the feast was, among the Latins on Cyprus, always approved by the Latin Church. It is also possible that this sentence refers, by anticipation, to the approval which Philippe obtained for it. Similarly, La Piana feels that the whole office, including the figurative representation, were a standard part of the liturgy on Cyprus, which Philippe merely recorded and presented to the Pope.

[4] Philippe may well have been in Venice from 1364 to 1368. He speaks here as if there were several performances of the Presentation Play before he presented it to the Pope.

Holy Pope Gregory of the said solemnity then unfortunately little known, shining in its blessings with new devotion, and presented the whole office to him humbly, along with the musical notations, asking of His Holiness, because of his devotion to the Virgin, that such a solemnity for the Mother of God, neglected and unknown in the West, being considered worthy, might be ordered to be celebrated everywhere in the lands of the apostolic authority, or at least be allowed to be celebrated at the will of the devotees. The same most holy Father Gregory—wisely watching out for those who are faithful, and mindful of the multiple harmony of the divine worship, like another David himself most singularly an imitation of the chosen all-holy, merciful in the highest and gracious in the flowers of chastity and humble in the zeal of the faith and fervent in devotion to Mary, not by any means abhoring the stammering tongue of the messenger nor scorning the leprous one drawing from the waters of the world, but touched and inflamed with love of the Virgin— worthily received the little book containing the aforesaid office with his own hands, and after many and most devout words of his own penetrating the fragile mind of the said chancellor because of their devoutness, the most Holy Father in concluding broke out in praise of the Virgin, saying: "There is no other remedy so efficacious for whatever sinner as to have recourse in all necessities to the Blessed Virgin Mary, and to hold to her service, and to praise her." Thus he said.

Then the most generous Pope, an enthusiast for the honor of Mary, having looked at the office in his own chamber, immediately afterwards with great urgency wished piously and catholically before the said chancellor that the said office be examined by other Most Reverend Fathers and Lords Cardinal and ordained Masters in the Sacred Page,[5] which was done; for the Bishop of Pamiers of sainted memory, the confessor of Pope Urban and of our Lord Pope Gregory, ordained Master in Theology of the Order of Hermits of Saint Augustine; and William Romain of the Order of Preaching Friars, also Master in the Sacred Page of the Sacred Palace, were the first to examine the said office. Afterwards the Most Reverend Lord

---

[5] The degree *Magister in Sacra Pagina* was the standard degree of a theologian until the thirteenth century, when it was gradually replaced by the degree *Magister in Theologicam*. The change in title was taken by some contemporaries, and has been considered by some modern scholars, as a change in emphasis from scriptural interpretation to logic; but it is clear from Philippe's exposition here that the Papal Court, and the various orders, liked to be supplied with Masters of both kinds.

Father Bertrand of Glandève, titled of Saint Priscus, Cardinal Priest, ordained Master in the Sacred Page of the Minor Order, examined the office at length and corrected some things in his own hand; then, besides, the Most Reverend Fathers the English Lord of Saint Albans, Cardinal Bishop, and Lord Peter of Seville, titled of Saint Praxid's, Cardinal Priest; and after these lords Brother Thomas the former Minister General of the Order of the Blessed Francis, now the Patriarch of Grado, Bishop of Châlons, Minister to France, Minister to Ireland, and Procurator of the Minor Order. All of the Masters of the Sacred Page gathered in one place looked at the said office, and in the presence of the said Most Reverend Lord Cardinal of Glandève not only approved the recognition of the said feast and office, but also recommended that it be celebrated immediately at the will of the devout everywhere. When a relation of all these things was made to His Holiness the Pope of our Lord, the most worthy vicar of the same and His imitator, who does not cease to honor His Mother on earth as should the most devout vicar the Mother of his Master, most prudent yet even more mature, and wishing to precede in this matter according to catholic practice, called to him several Lords Cardinal, and in consideration of the initial counsel and supplication of the aforesaid Chancellor, at that time finally set in motion the matter in this manner—the divine Clemency revealing the true honor of His Mother in the salvation and consolation of Christians and the glorious Virgin inspiring in his heart the vicar of her Son, to whom it was clearly of importance at that time and place to correct, modify, nourish, augment, and institute anew the divine worship—for this reason he conceded mercifully that the feast of the Presentation of the Blessed Mary in the Temple might be publicly celebrated in a short time before the pious faithful, as holy and as worthy of this encouragement and permission. And the feast of the Presentation of the Blessed Mary was observed in the Roman Curia with its proper office as described above, with the Most Blessed Pope Gregory giving it his permission and encouragement from the sacred palace at Avignon, in the church of the Friars Minor, more particularly on Sunday the twenty-first day of the month of November, the year of the Nativity of our Lord 1372, in the 150th pontificate of our Lord, the second year of Lord Pope Gregory the Eleventh.

And so for the vigil of that very Sunday, the Vespers for this feast, and with the passage of the night the Matins, were celebrated by the Friars Minor according to the set office. And on the scheduled Sunday a solemn and pontifical Mass was celebrated in the said church of the Blessed Francis by the Reverend Father Lord Bishop of Roman Cortona, ordained Master in the Sacred Page of the Order of Preachers, with a sermon on the same feast to the clergy in the Mass and a sermon in the vulgar tongue at the Second Vespers admirably delivered by Brother Francis de Fabrica, Minister of Assisi, ordained Doctor of Theology. Yet in addition, to honor the aforesaid feast of the Blessed Mary, the Most Reverend Fathers in Christ and Lords Cardinal listed below, all devoted to the Virgin, participated in the Mass: that is to say, the English Lord of Saint Albans, a Cardinal Bishop, brother of the former Pope Urban the Fifth of sainted memory; Lord Peter of Pampilona, titled of Saint Anastasia's, a Cardinal Priest and Vice-Chancellor of the Roman Church; Lord William, titled of Saint Clement's, a Cardinal Priest, related in blood to our Lord the Pope; Lord Peter of Florence, titled of Saint Laurence's *in Damaso*, a Cardinal Priest; Lord John of Limoges, titled of Saints Nereus and Achileus, a Cardinal Priest, relative of Our Lord the Pope; Lord Bertrand of Glandève, titled of Saint Priscus's, a Cardinal Priest; Lord John de la Tour, titled of Saint Laurence's *in Lucina*, a Cardinal Priest; Lord Hugh of Saint Martial, titled of Saint Mary's *in Porticu*, a Cardinal Deacon; and Lord Peter of Barentonio, titled of Saint Mary's in the Via Lata, a Cardinal Deacon. There were as well other lords and prelates of the Church, the Lord Patriarch of Grado, chief secretaries, archbishops, bishops, abbots, masters of the sacred palace, and other masters in theology of diverse orders, regents in the sacred page, doctors ordained in both laws, and the catholic populus of both sexes who were not numbered, all gathered together in new praise of the Virgin Mary and gloriously satiated in varying degrees with new spiritual food from the Virgin, carefully picked and prepared finally for the eternal life.

And no wonder, most dear Fathers and Brothers, that to such an extent in this holy feast, not lacking in mystery, can the devoted mind in contemplation be refreshed with a five-fold food and be satiated. For the first food can be said to be this translation[6] of Mary to be

---

[6] *Translatio* was the rite wherein the bones or other relics of a saint were brought to the church of which that saint was patron. Philippe regards Mary, even while living, as the "patron" of the whole Church, of which the temple in Jerusalem was the precursor.

made holy, although already most holy, at the age of three, from the house of her fleshly father to the house of her Father eternal God, from the obscurity of her parental cell to the notice of the people of Israel and to the hall of the King of the living. For if the Holy Church makes such a celebration for the translation of the bones of the dead, what ought she to do for the transfer of the most blessed Mary from her parental home to the temple of God? And the second food can be imaged with the eye of the mind, that is, Mary's mature ascent of the fifteen steps, for which reason, the church has adopted not inappropriately the fifteen Gradual Psalms in memory of the aforesaid ascension. And the saints in praise of the Virgin in song recite the fifteen joys of the most devout Virgin Mary. Then the third food, and in the feast our principal one, is the Presentation of the Blessed Mary in the Temple to God the Father itself. For it was certainly appropriate and fitting that she who from the beginning and before worldly time was ordained to conceive and bear in her womb the price of human redemption, God and man, be presented in the temple to God, where she might be instructed by the Holy Spirit in things divine, and be totally drawn away from the conversation and companionship of the world. Most surely delectable is this food, the contemplation of the preparation of our redemption in Mary. But the fourth food ought to inebriate virgins and chaste minds, Mary among others being presented in the temple to the high priest and withdrawn into the company of virgins, awaiting the redemption of Israel, being taught by the Holy Spirit, the first to vow virginity, which is pleasing to God, in the temple, in opposition to human custom, that she might become the Mother of the Son of God and not leave behind her virginity. And by all means the fifth food ought certainly to raise the devout mind from all things corporeal, in contemplating the whole life of Mary, her extraordinary acts and her virtues, from her presentation in the temple up to her thirteenth or fourteenth year, her most holy life always the same, giving light to the temple. For what is more worthy to be contemplated in the fullest than this divine dispensation and novelty, in which the Virgin Queen is led to marry the aged Joseph, the flowering staff approving Joseph and the Jewish people amazed?

And so all these mysteries and preparations for the coming of the Savior to Mary are acted in the temple in the following under the title of the Presentation, for which things the devout mind observing the sabbath today in the church of God rejoices in his heart. For this reason the Holy Fathers instituted this glorious feast not without great mystery nor unsuitable for the praise of God and the Virgin, in which they have set forth for us all of the mysteries of the beginning and the bases of our human redemption, all of which will be clearly apparent in the songs for the above-mentioned office of the Presentation set down for your devotions.

This scanty letter, disorderly and conceived without wit, along with the most devout office of the Presentation of Mary in the Temple, the aforesaid Chancellor, your little worm and an aborted zealot, decided to have sent for your greater devotion, Fathers and Lords of the west, center, and north of the catholic world, in order to excite the hearts of the faithful, particularly of the devotees of the Queen of Heaven, considering her the most worthy of these praises, not that from this he would acquire the vain wind of human praise, let the unspotted Virgin herself attest, but so that she inspiring and her Son perfecting, such celebration with the following signs would not remain concealed from your hearts; and he entreats humbly that however much, through your contemplation of this celebration in places of assembly, you are newly enraptured by Mary and affected by thanks, you will deign to intercede in your prayers with her to the same extent for the soul of your little worm, so that then all our Christians, with this multiplication of interceders, will merit to evade the broad sentences proceeding from the judgment of the highest wrath because of the intercession of the Blessed Mary, and will be able to attain to that blessed vision which, according to Augustine, to perceive is the end.[7] Which thing may the blessed fruit of Mary who lives, reigns, and commands through infinite world without end deign to grant to us.

[7] The observation that the achievement of the beatific vision was the end of human life is to be found in St. Augustine, *Sermo LII.vi, Patrologia Latina* 38:366.

The Latin Text

Epistola de solennitate Presentacionis Beate Marie in Templo et nouitate ipsius ad partes occidentales que celebratur xxi Nouembris.

Uniuersis in Domino fidelibus, maxime Christianis occidentalibus, Philippus de Maiserijs, Picardie miles infimus, regni Cypri indignus cancellarius vocatus, ac gloriose Virginis Marie zelator abortiuus, sentencias irati summi iudicis per Mariam euadere et ad vitam sempiternam peruenire, exclamare plerumque compellitur dolorem communem et mala gentis nostre in lucem ad memoriam reducere. Dicant igitur nunc cum lacrimis qui redempti sunt a Domino Ihesu: Ve nobis Christianis, rubor in facie et liuor infamie, quia non sunt occultata hodie a filijs alienigenarum infidelium qui in circuitu nostro sunt mala inexplicabilia Christianis adeo inflicta peccatis hec inpetrantibus. Quante nempe pestilentie, seditiones, mortalitates, guerre, proditiones, et hereses temporibus nostris insurrexerunt, maxime ad plagam occidentalem, patet intuenti.

Flagellauit etenim Deus et continue flagellat Christianos, qui ad mortem, qui ad gladium, qui ad famem et captiuitatem, Ieremia predicente, et vere cum Bernardo ad Ostiensem, Penestrinum, et Tusculanum cardinales scribente, hodie non immerito dici potest: Sapientiam vincit malicia, adduntur ubique cornua inpijs, et exarmatur iusticie zelus, et non est qui facere bonum, non dico velit, sed possit; superbi inique agunt usquequaque, et nullus audet contra mutire, et vtinam uel ignorantia tuta esset, et iusticia ipsa sibimet sufficeret defensioni. Hec ille.

Nec mirum, Patres et Fratres carissimi, quia, cum precibus nostris pulsamus redemptorem, non calescit, quia iratus est nobis; auertit faciem suam et conturbati sumus. Quid igitur fiendum est desperandum? Absit. Sed in tantis processis, flagellis et periculis secure ad portum salutis festinandum videlicet ad aduocatam peccatorum,

59

Mediatricem Dei et hominum, Reginam misericordie, et Matrem Dei, intemeratam Virginem Mariam Christiferam cum nouis laudibus vociferando reccurendum, ut videlicet sua pietas sinum sue misericordie nobis adaperiat, et in recensione iocunditatis laudum sue Presentationis deuocius allecta apud benedictum fructum ventris sui, Ihesum filium suum vnigenitum, pro miseria nostra ipsum placando plus solito intercedere dignetur, ut ipsa adiuuante et protegente a malis liberemur, ad viam rectam reducamur, et sine timore de manu inimicorum nostrorum liberati seruiamus illi deinceps in sanctitate et iusticia omnibus diebus nostris.

Cantemus igitur carmen nouum Regine celi, et antiquas laudes Marie Presentationis in Templo de partibus Orientis nouiter coruscantes vniuersis fratribus nostris Christianis in plaga occidentali, australi et septentrionali de gentibus pro antidoto et leticia spirituali annunciemus. Audiant ergo vniuersi Catholici Europe et Affrice, presertim deuoti intemerate Virginis, eius deuotissimam solennitatem utique in ecclesia occidentali nouam ac rutilantem in cordibus zelatorum Virginis, quamuis antiquam in ecclesia orientali, et ad nouam deuotionem excitentur. Temporibus namque antiquis, et, ut creditur, in primitia ecclesia quando ciuitas sancta Iherusalem et Terra Sancta per Christianos detinebatur, ibique in alijs partibus Orientis in quibus vigebat fides catholica, sanctis patribus instituentibus et verisimiliter miraculis declarantibus, festum Beatissime semper Virginis Marie, quando in tercio etatis sue anno in templo per seipsam quindecim gradibus templi miraculose ascensis, fuit in dicto templo a parentibus suis presentata, die xxi mensis Nouembris deuotissime et solempniter celebrabatur. Et adhuc in regno Cypri deuotissime per fideles Orientis colitur de presenti, et habet officium totum proprium et duotissimum secundum usum Curie Romane, etiam musice notatum.

Quod quidem festum supramemoratus cancellarius, quamuis indignus et inutilis, pre deuotione Virginis et iocunditate admirans et in corde suo pie extimans indignum quod tanta solennitas partes lateret occidentales, in quibus, protegente Domino, fidei plenitudo consistit, ob reuerentiam ipsius Beatissime semper Virginis, ipsa adiuuante, dictam solempnitatem iam pluribus annis elapsis in aliquibus partibus Ytalie, videlicet in preclara ciuitate Venetiarum, aliquibus electis deuote Virginis ipsius ciuitatis adiuuantibus, solempniter celebrari fecit cum representatione figurata et deuotissima, aliquibus signis et visionibus dictam solempnitatem de cetero celebrandam confirmantibus et eam communicantibus, de qua certe noua deuotio et iocunda Matris Dei in cordibus multorum fidelium non mediocriter exorta est.

Adueniente plerumque dicto cancellario ambassiatore serenissimi principis, Petri Iherusalem et Cypri regis iuuenculi filij, quondam armipotentis Machabei victoriosissime ac lacrimabilis memorie sui quondam domini pro factis orientalibus ad pedes Sanctissimi in Christo Patris et Domini Nostri Domini Gregorij Pape xi^{mi}, Sacrosancte Romane ac vniuersalis Ecclesie Summi Pontificis, toto nisu anhelante ut solennitas sepetacta Beate Marie semper Virginis ubique terrarum auctoritate apostolica diuulgaretur, et cum illa humilitate qua potiut, non qua debuit, et deuotione qualicumque oracionum tamen fultus multorum deuotorum Virginis utriusque sexus et adiutus non in arcu suo sperans sed in arcu celesti qui diuinam maiestatem inclinauit usque ad uterum virginalem, dicto Sanctissimo Pape Gregorio dictam solennitatem rutilantem noue deuotionis beatitudini sue tunc ignotam minus male annunciauit, ac officium integrum etiam musice notatum humiliter presentauit, supplicando eidem sanctitati, vice deuotorum Virginis, ut tanta solennitas Matris Dei, ab occidentalibus incognita et neglecta, ubique terrarum auctoritate apostolica celebrari mandare dignaretur, aut saltem deuotis volentibus celebrari permitteret. Qui quidem sanctissimus Pater Gregorius sane vigilans in hijs que fidei sunt, et recensione multiplici armonie diuini cultus, uelut alter Dauid ipsius panaye singulariter electus imitator, in summa clementia et mansuetudine in florida castitate et humilitate in zelo fidei et feruenti deuotione Marie, non utique annunciantis linguam balbutientem abhorrens seu leprosum haurientem aquam mundam repellens, sed amore Virginis tactus et inflammatus, libellum officij memorati manibus proprijs dignanter recepit, ac post multa et deuotissima uerba ipsius animam dicti cancellarij fragilem pre deuotione penetrantia, concludendo Sanctissimus Pater in laudem Virginis prorupit dicens: Non est aliquod remedium ita efficax cuicumque peccatori sicut recursum habere in omni necessitate ad Beatam Virginem Mariam, eique adherere sibi seruire et ipsam laudare. Hec ille.

Tandem clementissimus Papa zelator honoris Marie, viso officio in studio proprio, inportunitate dicti cancellarii postea prosequente voluit pie et catholice sepetactum officium per aliquos reuerendissimos patres et dominos cardinales ac magistros in sacra pagina solempnes examinari debere, quod et factum est, nam Episcopus Pamiensis sancte memorie, Vrbani Pape ac Domini Nostri Gregorij Pape confessor, solempnis in theologia magister Ordinis Heremitarum Sancti Augustini, et Guilielmus Romani Ordinis Fratrum Predicatorum etiam in sacra pagina magister Sacri Palacij, primo examinauerunt dictum officium. Deinde Reuerendissimus Pater Dominus Bertrandus Glandatensis, tituli Sancte Prisce, Presbyter Cardinalis, solempnis magister in sacra pagina de Ordine Minorum officium prolixe examinauit et aliqua propria manu correxit; deinde etiam Reuerendissimi Patres Dominus Anglicus Albanensis, Episcopus Cardinalis, et Dominus Petrus Hyspalensis, tituli Sancte Praxedis, Presbyter Cardinalis; post istos vero dominos Frater Thomas quondam Minister Generalis Ordinis Beati Francisci, nunc vero Patriarcha Gradiensis, Episcopus Cauilonensis, Minister Francie, Minister Hibernie, et Procurator Ordinis Minorum. Omnes magistri in sacra pagina insimul congregati dictum officium viderunt, et in presentia reuerendissimi dicti Domini Cardinalis Gladatensis non solum dictam sollennitatem et officium approbauerunt sollennizandum, sed etiam ut celebrari debeat a deuotis volentibus ubique instanter intercesserunt. Factaque relatione de omnibus ad sanctitatem Domini Nostri Pape, idem vicarius dignissimus et imitator illius, qui non cessat Matrem honorare in terris quamius deuotissimus vicarius Matris sui magistri prudentissimus tamen maturius et catholice in hac parte procedere volens, quam plures dominos cardinales ad se vocauit, et inito consilio supplicationeque dicti cancellarij, hic inde ventilata tandem diuina clementia honorem Matris in salutem et consolacionem Christianorum verisimiliter reuelante ac Virgine gloriosa in corde vicarij filij sui inspirante, cui plane interest pro tempore et loco cultum diuinum corrigere, modificare, tollerare, augmentare, et de nouo instituere, celebrandi deinceps publice sollempnitatem Presentationis Beate Marie in Templo a fidelibus pie, sancte et digne tollerantiam seu permissionem misericorditer concessit; et facta est solempnitas Presentationis Beate Marie cum officio suo proprio sepetacto in Curia Romana, Beatissimo Papa Gregorio tollerante ac in sacro palatio suo degente Auinionensi in ecclesia Fratrum Minorum, videlicet die dominica xxi. die mensis Nouembris, anno de Natiuitate Domini m⁰. ccc⁰. lxxij., indictione decima pontificatus Domini Nostri Domini Gregorii Pape xiᵐˡ anno secundo.

In vigilia namque ipsius dominice Vespere sollemnes, et de nocte Matutine de officio prelibato per Fratres Minores celebrate fuerent.

Et dominica pretacta Missa solempnis et pontificalis in dicta ecclesia Beati Francisci celebrata fuit per Reuerendum Patrem Dominum Episcopum Cortonensem Romanum, magistrum in sacra pagina solempnem de Ordine Predicatorum, cum sermone eiusdem solennitatis ad clerum in Missa et predicatione vulgari in Vesperis Secundis ad populum laudabiliter factis per Fratrem Franciscum de Fabrica, ministrum Assisij solempnem doctorem in theologia. Verumptamen ad honorandam prelibatam solennitatem Beate Marie in Missa interfuerunt deuoti Virginis Reuerendissimi in Christo Patres et Domini Cardinales infrascripti, videlicet Dominus Anglicus Albanensis Episcopus Cardinalis, frater quondam sancte memorie Vrbani Pape Quinti, Dominus Petrus Pampilonensis, tituli Sancte Anastasie, Presbyter Cardinalis et Vice-cancellarius Ecclesie Roman, Dominus Guilielmus, tituli Sancti Clementis, Presbyter Cardinalis, consanguineus germanus Domini Nostri Pape, Dominus Petrus Florentinus, tituli Sancti Laurentij in Damasco, Presbyter Cardinalis, Dominus Iohannes Lemouicensis, tituli Sanctorum Nerey et Achilley, Presbyter Cardinalis, consanguineus Domini Nostri Pape Dominus Bertrandus Glandatensis, tituli Sancte Prisce, Presbyter Cardinalis, Dominus Iohannes de Turre, tituli Sancti Laurentij in Lucina, Presbyter Cardinalis, Dominus Hugo Sancti Martialis, tituli Sancte Marie in Porticu, Dyaconus Cardinalis, et Dominus Petrus de Barentonio, tituli Sancte Marie in Via Lata, Dyaconus Cardinalis. Fuerunt insuper alij domini et prelati ecclesie, Dominus Patriarcha Gradensis, prothonotarij, archiepiscopi, episcopi, abbates, magistri sacri palacij, et alij magistri in theologia diuersarum religionum, regentes in sacra pagina, doctores sollennes vtriusque iuris, ac catholicus populus utriusque sexus, quorum non erat numerus, omnes congregati in laudem nouam Virginis Marie gloriose saciati plerumque nouo spirituali cibo a Virgine exquisito et preparato finaliter in vitam eternam.

Nec mirum, Patres et Fratres karissimi, quia plerumque in ista sancta solempnitate, misterio non carente, mens deuota contemplando quintuplici cibo refici potest et saciari. Primus namque cibus dici potest quedam translatio Marie santificate, ymmo sanctissime, trium annorum de domo patris carnalis ad domum eterni Dei Patris, de tenebris cellule parentum ad ostensionem populi Israel et aulam regis viuentium. Si igitur ecclesia sancta de translatione ossium mortuorum tantam celebritatem facit, quid fiendum est de translatione Marie beatissime domus paterne ad Domini Templum? Secundus vero cibus ymaginari potest oculo mentali, videlicet matura ascensio Marie quindecim graduum, de quibus non immerito ecclesia quindecim psalmos graduales in memoriam ascensionis prelibate sibi assumpsit. Ac sancti laudatores Virginis in suis carminibus quindecim gaudia Virginis Marie deuotius recitarunt. Tercius autem cibus, et in sollennitate nostra principalis, est ipsa Presentatio Beate Marie in Templo ad Deum Patrem. Congruum nempe et conueniens erat, ut illa que ab initio et ante secula ordinata erat ad concipiendum et portandum in vtero pretium humane redemptionis, Deum et hominem, in templo Deo presentaretur, ibique a Spiritu Sancto de diuinis instrueretur et a conuersacione et contubernio mundanorum totaliter abstraheretur. Delectabilis est certe cibus iste contemplantibus preparationem redemptionis nostre in Maria. Sed quartus cibus virgines et mentes castas inebriare debet, Maria plerumque presentata in templo summo pontifici et reducta in contubernio virginum, expectans redemptionem Israel, contra morem humanum a Spiritu Sancto edocta in templo prima virginitatem vouit, quod tantum Deo placuit, ut Mater Filij Dei fierit et virginitatem non amitteret. Quintus plerumque cibus mentem deuotam ab omni corpore releuare certe debet contemplando totam vitam Marie, singulares actus, et virtutes ipsius a presentatione ipsius in templo usque ad annum tredecimum uel quartumdecimum sanctissima vita sua continue ibidem in templo relucente. Quis enim plene contemplari valet diuinam illam dispensationem atque nouitatem, in qua Virgo regia seni Ioseph nuptui traditur, florente virga Ioseph approbante et Iudaico populo admirante?

Omnia etenim ista misteria et preparatoria aduentus Saluatoris in Mariam in templo subsequenter acta sunt, de quibus omnibus sub titulo Presentationis hodie in ecclesia Dei mens deuota sabbatizando in corde iubilat. Igitur sancti patres non sine magno misterio solennitatem istam gloriosam, nec immerito ad laudem Dei et Virginis instituerunt, in qua nobis proponuntur tot misteria principia et fundamenta humane redemptionis nostre, que omnia in carminibus officij prelibate Presentacionis vestre deuocioni lucidius apparebunt.

Istam modicam epistolam incompositam ac sine sale conditam, cum deuotissimo officio Presentationis Marie in Templo, Patres et Domini catholici occidentales, meridionales, et septentrionales, memoratus cancellarius vermiculus vester et zelator abortiuus deuotioni vestre mitti decreuit, ad excitandum corda fidelium maxime deuotorum Regine Celi, necnon ad recensendum ipsius laudes dignissimas, non ut inde ventum humane laudis acquirat, ipsa intemerata Virgine teste, sed ut ipsa inspirante et Filio suo consumante, sequentibus signis in cordibus vestris tanta solennitas non lateat, et quandoque in consistorio contemplacionis vestre solennitatis noue in Mariam rapti et affecti per gratiam pro anima vestri vermiculi uestra deuocio quandoque apud ipsam intercedere dignetur humiliter exorat, vt etiam multiplicatis intercessoribus latas sentencias irati summi iudicis per intercessionem Beate Marie semper Virginis Christiani nostri euadere mereantur, et ad illam beatissimam visionem, cuius secundem Augustinum, cernere finis est, peruenire valeant. Quod nobis concedere dignetur fructus Marie benedictus qui viuit, regnat, et inperat per infinita secula seculorum. Amen.

The Note

Next: for the sake of the refreshing consolation of the devotees of the Most Blessed Virgin Mary, who have devoutly celebrated and will celebrate in the future, with rejoicing, the aforesaid feast of the Presentation of this Virgin in the Temple.

Let it be known that in the Year of our Lord 1385 in the city of Avignon, with the above-mentioned Philippe de Mézières, Chancellor of the King of Cyprus, personally handling the matter for our Lord the Highest Pontiff Clement the Seventh—this highest pontiff, not without devotion and reverence for the Mother of God, not only allowing, but devoutly ordaining it—the aforesaid feast of the Presentation of the Virgin by her parents in the temple was celebrated most devoutly and solemnly with a pontifical Mass on the twenty-first of November in the said year in the church of the Hermit Friars of the Blessed Augustine in Avignon, with eighteen cardinals, archbishops, and bishops, along with the whole clergy of the city of Avignon and the whole population of both sexes present to the end of the Mass. In which Mass, for the praise of the Virgin and for the sake of her devotees, was performed a certain representation with fifteen very young virgins of three of four years of age, of which one of the prettiest played Mary in the company of the said virgins. These, in various costumes, made a most devout procession, with Joachim and Anna acted out and with angels preceding and following the Virgin. Mary was led with the music of instruments to the altar, where she quickly ascended the fifteen wooden steps leading to the altar, and was figuratively presented by her parents and devoutly accepted by the high priest of the law of the Old Testament dressed in the habit of the highest pontiff of the Jews. Having been presented at the altar with the accompaniment of praises and davidic songs chanted in a loud voice by the angels Joachim, Anna, and Mary herself, she was led back to the middle of the choir and seated with the cardinals in a higher place as has been described, where she remained until the end of the celebration of the Mass, in which Mass, at the time of the offertory, the reverend and wondrously learned Master John of Basilia, the most highly ordained Doctor in Theology of the Teutonic nation and the General of the order of Hermit Friars of the Blessed Augustine, preached to the Lords Cardinal and the clergy concerning the holy feast of the Presentation of Mary in the Temple. The General made this sermon at the insistent request of our Lord the Highest Pontiff (though he had only three days for the provision of the sermon, nor were those complete); yet nevertheless it confirmed the devout heart, transformed through grace, in the love of the Virgin (and, as we see that so much solemnity will not remain hidden, why should it not be celebrated everywhere in the world from this time forth by all the faithful), the Virgin herself inspiring this General, a virgin in spirit; and the whole clergy and the lords cardinals gave public witness of this; they all, as in one voice, said that never in their time had they heard a more beautiful sermon on the Blessed Virgin in the Roman Curia. Afterwards our Lord Pope Clement the Seventh, kindled with devotion to the Virgin Mary and her devout feast, mercifully granted for the aforesaid divine office and feast to all present three years and three times forty days of indulgence, and one who heard and saw narrated gives testimony, and this testimony is true in the praise of the Mother of God and her blessed Son, who is blessed in the world without end.

The Latin Text

Item pro refricacione consolacionis deuotorum Beatissime Uirginis Marie qui sepetactam solempnitatem Presentacionis ipsius Uirginis in templo deuote celebrarunt et in futurum iubilando celebrabunt.

Notandum est quod Anno Domini millesimo trecentesimo octogesimo quinto in ciuitate Auinionensi, superius tacto Philippo de Maserijs, regni Cipri cancellario, personaliter procurante apud Dominum Nostrum Summum Pontificem Clementem Septimum, ipso summo pontifice non sine deuocione et reuerencia ipsius Matris Dei non solum permittente sed deuote ordinante pretacta solempnitas Presentacionis ipsius Uirginis a parentibus in templo xxj die Nouembris anni pretacti in ecclesia Fratrum Heremitarum Beati Augustini Auinioni deuotissime ac solempniter celebrata fuit cum Missa pontificali, vtique presentibus usque ad finem Misse xviij cardinalibus, archiepiscopis, episcopis cum vniuersali clero ipsius ciuitatis Auenionensis totoque populo vtriusque sexus. In qua quidem Missa solempni, ad laudem Uirginis deuocionemque suorum deuotorum, facta fuit quedam representacio xv iuuencularum uirginum trium aut quatuor annorum, quarum vna formosior representabat Mariam associatam a dictis uirginibus, et sic varijs indutis cum processione deuotissima cum Ioachim et Anna figuratis et angelis precedentibus Virginem ac sequentibus, ducta fuit cum instrumentis musicorum ad altare, ibique velox ascendit xv gradus ligneos tendetes ad altare et presentata a parentibus fuit figuraliter, et deuote accepta a summo sacerdote legis Veteris Testamenti induto habitu summorum pontificum Iudeorum. Qua presentata ad altare cum laudibus et carminibus dauiticis alta voce per angelos, Ioachim et Annam et ipsam Mariam recitatis, reducta est in medio chori, et cardinalium in loco eminenciori ut tactum est, associata, ibique expectauit usque ad finem Misse celebrate, in qua quidem Missa hora offertorij de sancta solempnitate

Presentacionis Marie in templo predicauit ad dominos cardinales et ad clerum reuerendus et in scientia admirabilis magister Iohannes de Basilia, solempnissimus doctor in theologia Theothonicus nacione ac generalis ordinis Fratrum Heremitarum Beati Augustini, qui quidem generalis de mandato viue vocis Domini Nostri Summi Pontificis, fecit sermonem, nec habuit spacium prouidendi sermonem pretactum nisi tres dies nec completos et tamen ad confirmandum cor deuotum transformatum per gratiam in amorem Uirginis, ut videlicet tanta solempnitas non lateat quin ymo a fidelibus vbique terrarum deinceps celebretur, ipsa Uirgine uirginum in animam ipsius generalis mirabiliter inspirante sequentibus signis toto clero et dominis cardinalibus publice attestantibus quasi vna voce omnes dicebant quod numquam temporibus ipsorum pulcriorem sermonem de Beata Uirgine audiuerant in Curia Romana. Denique ipse Dominus Noster Papa Clemens Septimus, deuocione Uirginis Marie eiusque deuota solempnitate accensus, in pretacto diuino officio et festiuitate omnibus existentibus tres annos et tres quadregenas indulgenciarum misericorditer concessit, et qui audiuit et narrata vidit testimonium perhibuit, et verum est testimonium eius ad laudem Matris Dei Filijque eius benedicti, qui est benedictus in secula seculorum.

Mary's Early Life
from Philippe's
Book of the Sacrament
of Marriage

This translation has been made from my own edition of a passage from Philippe de Mézières's Livre du Sacrament de Mariage et du reconfort des dames mariées. *It can be noted even in English translations that Philippe's style in French was much the same as his style in Latin. For the ladies who could not read Latin and who were therefore likely to be less learned than the intended readers of the Presentation Play, Philippe's figures of speech are even more extravagant and his self-depreciation more extreme. But, in content and method, this work has much in common with the play. Philippe's retelling of Mary's early life, his redaction of the apocryphal gospels in which this life is recorded, is legendary rather than dramatic and symbolic. But he takes care to place this life in the context of history and doctrine, so that it manifests the same providential purposes referred to by the angels in the* laudes *for Mary. Philippe assumes that his audience of married ladies will see in the symbolic and allegorical significance of this life applications to their private sacramental condition just as the audience of the Presentation Play is asked to find applications to their public congregational life.*

The edition of the passage, which follows the translation, is readable rather than authoritative. I have silently emended the original text to bring the punctuation, accenting, word-division, and even in a few instances the spelling into accord with modern practice. In all other respects, however, I have left the wording of the text as it stands. The principal manuscript of the Book of the Sacrament of Marriage *is, like the one containing the Presentation Play, in Philippe's own hand. A portion of this manuscript, its retelling of the story of Griselde, has been edited in Élie Golenistcheff-Koutouzoff,* L'histoire de Griseldis en France au XIVᵉ et au XVᵉ siècle (*Paris: Droz, 1933*). *The Manuscript, BN fr. 1175, is described on pp. 34–35 of that book, and the illumination at the beginning of the manuscript has been used by M. Golenistcheff-Koutouzoff for his frontispiece. He has also published a later study:* Étude sur Le livre de la vertue du sacrament de mariage et reconfort des dames mariées de Philippe de Mézières (*Belgrade: Svetlost, 1937*).

73

The Presentation of the Virgin Mary

The passage I have edited is to be found between fols. 42ʳ and 45ʳ of the manuscript, at the beginning of the second section. In section I, Philippe has retold the story of the Crucifixion, which is the wedding of Christ and the Church; this is the "tearful wedding" to which he refers in section II. In sections III and IV he has promised to deal with the marriage of God and the reasonable soul, and with the marriage of man and woman respectively. (It is in section IV that the story of Griselde is found.) Each of these literal or symbolic marriages is said to unite a fine ruby with a fine diamond, and to constitute one face of a mirror of marriage; these two figures of speech are often referred to in the passage which follows.

It should be clear in even this short excerpt that this work has interest beyond the light it sheds on the Presentation Play. It derives its figures of speech from other fourteenth-century writers; for example, the Mirror of Marriage *was the title of a poem by Deschamps. And, in the concern it shows for ladies who have learned to read the vernacular and to enjoy learned discourse, it shows Philippe's attentiveness to an audience which other writers were discovering as well; see, for instance, the Prologue to Boccaccio's* Decameron. *Most importantly, in taking marriage as a prime sacrament and mystery and as an object of moral and theological focus, it shows Philippe's affinity with other writers for whom marriage had become a central literary theme, such as not only Deschamps but also Chaucer in his so-called discussion of marriage in the* Canterbury Tales; *Gower in his* Cinquante Ballades; *and Christine de Pisan in* L'Avision.

Mary's Early Life

Here begins the second section and the second face of the mirror explained in the Prologue. Concerning the fine diamond joined to the fine ruby by the sacrament of spiritual marriage; concerning the most sweet virgin Mary sweetly representing our Mother Holy Church, queen and bride of the tearful wedding described above; concerning the conditions and virtues of her nativity; and concerning her holy life and how God made her beautiful, holy, and clean, so as to be mother and bride of his blessed son, Jesus Christ.

The First Chapter of the Second Section

Now it is time, God willing, to enter into the matter, both joyous and piteous, of the mother and singular bride of our fine ruby, the Virgin Mary, representing our mother, Holy Church, as was described above. For concerning her, her condition, and her great estate, and concerning her particular queenly majesty, as these pertain to the marriage mentioned above or to the nuptials to be described, there has been little or nothing yet written. And because the pen raised up by this vile and old writer is quite stained and badly constructed, I pray devoutly to the Queen of Nuptials who by her consenting alone was able to write in her womb the King of Heaven that she, out of her sweet mercy, would be pleased to sharpen this crude and gross pen, to efface completely its stains, and to form a pen entirely to her liking, so that this writer may write something suitable to the praise of the King of Nuptials, and of the Holy Queen, who aids the writer and to the consolation as well of married people, of all good Christians, and in particular of married ladies and of that one for which this matter, such as it is, was undertaken.

Now, let it be known, there are two things in particular which should be established concerning this powerful queen. The first of these is her particular condition when she came to the alliance of marriage, and the great joy which came into the world, particularly to her parents and to her race, because of the aforesaid alliance of marriage. This first matter is in confirmation of the earlier chapter which discussed the sacrament of marriage between the blessed Son of God, Jesus Christ, and our humanity. The second thing which should be established is the condition of our most sweet queen with reference to the nuptials and their provisions. And, as for the first, let it be directly declared that it was a reasonable and fitting thing for the Great King of Kings, Son of the All-Powerful God, who through his grace had determined to make alliance by means of the sacrament of marriage with our poor and very vile nature, to take as bride, as mother, and as queen of nuptials a lady of high lineage who, in beauty, in goodness, in purity, and in all virtues, exceeded all the ladies of the world. So however much the readers of this treatise on marriage already have full knowledge of this noble lady— and blessed are the men and women who know her well and follow her devoutly—we should still not hesitate to set down once again the graces and conditions of this powerful queen through whom so much good has come to our race. Then let us now enter into the matter.[1]

There was once a noble baron of Israel, rich, powerful, and fearing God, with the privileges of a priest,[2] whose name was Joachim. He had a companion and wife equal to his conditions named Anna,

[1] The sources of the account which follows are three apocryphal gospels which are themselves probably based upon some common source, since they vary from each other only in style and in certain unimportant details. *The Book of James* (called in modern times the *Protevangelium*) was attributed to James the apostle, while the *Gospel of Pseudo-Matthew* (or *Liber de Infantia*) was accompanied by letters purporting to have been sent to and from Saint Jerome, describing how the gospel was written and translated. The *Gospel of the Birth* (or *Nativity*) *of Mary* was also attributed to Saint Jerome and included among his works; it was included in full in Jacobus de Voragine's *Golden Legend*. Translations of these apocrypha can be conveniently found in B. Harris Cowper, *The Apocryphal Gospels* (London: David Nutt, 1910), and later editions; and in M. R. James, *The Apocryphal New Testament* (Oxford: Clarendon Press, 1924), and later editions. Cowper has complete translations of all three sources. James has complete translations of *The Book of James* and of the letters to and from Saint Jerome which preface the *Gospel of Pseudo-Matthew*, but has only outlines and excerpts from this gospel and from the *Gospel of the Birth of Mary*.

[2] None of the sources say that Joachim was a priest. Rather he is explicitly said to be a rich sheep-herder who was scrupulously generous in his gifts and sacrifices.

who was an old woman but had never borne fruit, which was a great sorrow to them both. And thus they were twenty years without descendants, for which reason Joachim, once when he was performing his office in the temple and offering sacrifice, was rudely thrown out by the Chief Priest of the Jews since he had not engendered fruit in Israel, saying that he was not worthy to offer sacrifice to God. Joachim left, confused and dishonored, and went out among his shepherds and beasts for around thirty days in order to escape the embarrassment, while Anna remained in Nazareth, confused and full of shame.[3]

A long time earlier they had made an oath to God that, if he would provide them with fruit of their lineage, they would present it to the service of God. This gracious story has been treated at length by Saint Jerome,[4] so definitively that I may abridge my writing, and say that following a message from an angel brought to Joachim and to Anna, Joachim returned to his house, and Anna conceived the most sweet Virgin Mary, who was sanctified in the womb of her mother to an incomparably greater extent than ever any other purely human creature, and was preserved and born pure, holy, and clean, and with the kindling, which is the spur of sin, both venial and mortal, killed in her, as has never been granted to any other purely created being.[5]

Note this marvel, that the Creator of all creatures uniquely created this noble vessel to receive and give a home in itself to the Bread of Life which gives life to angels and men; it became his own body; and in this precious vessel to the great wonder and unequaled joy of our race the nuptials so often referred to above were solemnly

---

[3] Joachim's expulsion by the chief priest is recorded in all the sources, as is his retirement among his shepherds. This story is clearly based upon the Old Testament narratives which tell of the birth of children to women (Sarah, Rachel) who had been sterile until old age, and of the special dedication of children (Samson, Samuel) who were born under unusual circumstances; all of these are alluded to in chapter III of the *Gospel of the Birth of Mary*.

[4] Saint Jerome is not only the alleged translator of the *Gospel of the Birth of Mary* and of the *Gospel of Pseudo-Matthew;* he is also said to be the translator of two other apocrypha surviving from the fourteenth century and edited by M. R. James, *Latin Infancy Gospels* (Cambridge: Cambridge University Press, 1927).

[5] The apocryphal gospels only hint at the idea of the Immaculate Conception; see chapter III of the *Gospel of the Birth of Mary*.

celebrated.[6] What more can I say concerning our young queen about her beauty, her goodness, about the virtues and graces granted to her? I cannot describe adequately even my conception of the virtues of the Queen of Heaven, for my pen is not well enough constructed. Even were all the waters of the seas to become ink, all the plains of Syria, parchment, and all the trees of the forest[7] to become pens, there would not be room for a description of the thousandth of a thousandth part of them; nor can they be clarified by comparison, for any thing to which they might be compared would be in quality or quantity like a single drop of water to the whole ocean. I must then describe, through her grace, what I can, not what I ought, and hope that, for her part, she will of her sweet goodness take little or nothing as the expression of good will.

Returning now to our matter: when the sweet girl and virgin was weaned from the breast, and was three years old, Joachim and Anna presented her in the temple, thus fulfilling their oath to God. And at the presentation of the little Virgin Mary, who was only three years old, she climbed, all by herself and without any human aid, the fifteen steps of the temple, which were both steep and wide, and so easily and so vigorously that the Chief Priest as well as the others who saw her were so amazed at it that they were quite certain that this young virgin belonged to God. Thus her father and her mother left their daughter in the service of God in the company of the virgin daughters of the great barons of Israel who were raised in the temple. And the manner in which our young queen, the sweet Virgin Mary, was brought up in the temple should be made known, for the angels rejoiced at it.

According to Saint Jerome's narrative, Mary, of her own volition and by the grace of the Holy Spirit who gently governed her, so arrɛ ɪged her life that from dawn to the third hour she was occupied in unbroken prayer, while from the third to the ninth hour she labored with her beautiful hands, making silk veils and other things pertaining to the service of God in the temple. She took no break from this work until an angel came down from heaven and imparted to her her bodily sustenance. After this sustenance, she returned once again to her prayers, so that she would not miss her works

[6] That is, the marriage of God with our humanity.

[7] The French text speaks of "la forest du biere," which may be some specific forest (of Bavaria?).

of mercy. She offered up to God the food which was distributed to her every day by the priests of the law. Thus she ate nothing except what the angel brought her. And according to what Saint Jerome and Saint Ambrose say,[8] she was never noted to be idle while either reading or listening to the law of God, or while occupied in prayer and contemplation, or while sewing vestments for the divine office. In addition, she did with great humility what the older ladies of the temple would not do, and often reprimanded the other virgins, her companions dwelling in the temple, when she saw them laugh too much or do or say any dishonest thing.

In brief, according to what the saints say, from the time when she entered the temple at the age of only three years she seemed so wise and so well-behaved that she might have been thirty years of age. And although in scriptural law a curse is placed on anyone of the people of Israel who does not bear fruit to God in marriage, nevertheless our sweet Virgin Mary, inspired by holiness, in order to better please God, vowed virginity and became the first to do so. Note this marvel: the angels so governed her and the Holy Spirit so instructed her in the law of God and in her duties that, when she came to understand perfectly the writings of the prophets, upon reading the prophesy of Isaiah concerning the virgin who was to conceive Messiah, the redeemer of the world, along with those other prophecies which pertain to this virgin, the sweet Virgin Mary then found herself so transported that, not without tears of devotion, she prayed sweetly to God that she might see this virgin and serve her by washing her feet. Such a supreme humility reigned in her that she would never have dared to think or imagine for herself that she might be this virgin promised in the law by whom the world was to be ransomed.[9]

She was always the first and the last during canonical hours to recite the psalms of David and the other prophecies; and no one ever saw her laugh in saying some idle word. She blessed God

[8] The reference here is to a passage from Saint Ambrose, *De virginibus*, used as a reading in the office of the Feast of the Presentation. The passage does not, however, make reference to Mary's dwelling in the temple; it rather seems to assume she is living at home. See Kishpaugh, *The Feast of the Presentation*, pp. 64–65.

[9] This story of her refusing to believe that the passages in Isaiah refer to herself is Philippe's own addition to the legend, not to be found in any of the sources.

without intermission: in order that the name of God would not be out of her mouth when someone greeted her, she responded as her greeting, "Thanks be to God."[10] Note this marvel: the angels were so familiar with her that night and day they were with her, guarding, honoring, and serving her. Never was there such a virgin nor will there be, and most blessed is he who would love her sweetly.

It was the custom among the People of God of Israel that the daughters of princes, barons, and lords be raised in the temple up to the time that they were of marriageable age, in order that they might be kept well; and when they were ready for marriage, the chief priests of the law sent them back, with solemnity, to the dwellings of their parents. But when the time came that our virgin (whom I have had to, most pleasantly, mention so often) was thirteen and of marriageable age, along with the other virgins who had been brought up with her in the temple, and when the chief priest decreed that these virgins should return to their parents in order to be given in marriage, the sweet Virgin Mary alone responded to the effect that she could not do it, and this for two reasons. In the first place, because her father and mother had vowed her perpetually to God, and in the second place because she had vowed virginity and dedicated it to the service of God.

When the Chief Priest heard the sweet Virgin Mary speak in this manner, he was completely confused and did not know what to reply to the virgin, fearing on the one hand to go against the writing of the prophet David who said, "Make an oath to God, and render unto God your oaths."[11] On the other hand he feared introducing a new custom into the law of Moses, that is to say, that young girls might remain virgins and thus not bear fruit nor increase the number of the people of God. In this dilemma he consulted the elders of the law, and it was determined that in a case of such novelty it would be expedient to seek the counsel of God. He, through a voice from heaven, commanded that the said virgin be married and put into the hands of the aged Joseph who was by direct line descended from the lineage of David, as was clear from the public record. I will now pass over the flowering of Joseph's rod, the descending of a dove from on high, and the other miracles which happened on this

[10] According to the sources, Mary was the originator of the greeting "*Deo gracias.*"

[11] Psalm 26:4. See also Deuteronomy 23:21 and Ecclesiastes 5:4.

occasion, for the sake of brevity and because they are common knowledge.[12]

The sweet Virgin Mary, as has been said, was joined by the sacrament of spiritual marriage to the holy aged man Joseph. She was his true spouse according to the law while remaining a virgin, and Joseph also as a virgin remained her true spouse. The betrothal having been made in the temple, as described, Joseph went off to his city of Bethlehem, that is, to the city to which he belonged as a result of belonging to the house and lineage of David who was from Bethlehem, in order to prepare everything which was necessary for the nuptials between him and Mary to be celebrated in the temple at a set time. The most blessed and elect virgin of God, Mary, accompanied by seven other virgins whom the chief priest had chosen to accompany her, who had been brought up with her in the temple, went off directly toward her parents in Nazareth where she was born.

And, for our consolation, this should not be left out: when the sweet and tender Virgin Mary was at the point of departure from the temple along with the seven other virgins already mentioned, these virgins who were with Mary agreed to cast lots in a friendly contest in order to determine, through the lots and through the will of God, which one from among all of the said virgins would be their leader, having governance of the others and perhaps relieving of her labor our sweet Mary, who was tender of body and did not have strength to walk on foot or to labor too hard. The virgins then put down as lots eight kerchiefs, which were pieces of flaxen or silk clothes of various colors, among which was a silken cloth of a reddish color known as purple. It was agreed among the virgins that the one who drew the purple would be their queen; and, in short, when the drawing took place, the purple fell by chance, but according to God's ordinance, to the sweet Virgin Mary. So the virgins from that time on called Mary their queen; and thus for the first time she was called by the name, Queen of the Virgins. According to the story of this gracious matter, an angel appeared in their midst and confirmed the name of Queen of the Virgins, both in heaven and on earth, to the sweet Virgin Mary.

[12] The story varies in all the sources, but the essential details are the same. A voice from heaven tells the priests (or a drawing of lots tells them) to choose a husband from the house of David. All the unmarried (or widowed) men of that house place rods in the Holy of Holies; Joseph's, which had been originally left out, flowers, and a dove flies from the end of it and rests upon Joseph. He at first tries to refuse, but is told that God is quite harsh on those who resist such divine signs.

The French Text

Cy commence le secont livre et la seconde face du miroir au prologue proposé. C'est du fin diamant conjoint au fin rubin par sacrament de mariage spirituel. C'est de la tresdoulce vièrge Marie, doulcement représentant nostre mère Saincte Esglise, reyne et espouse des noces lacrimables dessus récitées; de ses condicions, et vertus de sa nativité, et de sa sancte vie; et comment Dieu la fist belle, saincte et nette pour estre mère et espouse de son bénoît fil, Jhesucrist.

Le prémier chapitre du second livre

Or il est temps, au nom de Dieu, d'entrer en la matère, et joyeuse et piteuse, de la Mère et Espouse Singulère de nostre fin rubin, de la poissant reyne des noces proposées, la trèsdoulce Vierge Marie, représentant nostre mère, Saincte Église, comme pardessûs fû promis. Car de lui, de sa condicion, ni de son grant estat, ni de sa maiesté réginale en espécial, comme il appendroit au mariage dessus dit, ne aux noces proposées, ou paou ou moins que à devotion, a ésté saincte mencion. Et parceque la penne aprît de cestui vil et viel escripnam est (bien grâce) soulié et mautaillié, je souplie dévotement â la reyne des noces, qui, par son seul consentment, sot escripre en son ventre le roy du firmament, que, par sa doulce pitié, la penne desusdicte, rude et grosse, elle veuille à soutiller, et ses soulliures entièrement efacier, et la dicte penne doulcement à son voloir taillier, afin que l'escripnam puisse escripre chose qui soit à la loenge du poissant roy des noces, et de la sainte reyne adrecant l'escripnam, à consolacion ausi des mariés, et de tout bon crestien; et par éspecial des dames mariées, et de celle pour laquelle ceste matère, telement quelement, est emprise.

Dont, il est à savoîr que de ceste poissant reyne deux choses en especial nons avons à veoir. La première si est de sa condicion par-

ticulère quant à l'aliance du mariage proposé, et de la grant joie
qui vint au monde, et par espécial à ses parens, et à sa généracion,
par la grant aliance du mariage proposé: ceste première partie est
confirmation du chapitre cy-dessus, qui traite briefment du sacrament
de mariage du bénoît fils de Dieu, Jesucrist, à nostre humanité.
La seconde chose que nous devons veoir si est de la condicion de
nostre trésdoulce reyne quant aux noces proposées, et à leur dépen-
dantes. Et quant à la première, il est à savoîr, briefment, que raison-
nable chose estoît, et affréable, que le grant roy des roys, fil de Dieu
tout poissant, que par sa grâce avoit determiné de faire aliance, par
sacrement de mariage, à nostre povre et très vile nature, présist pour
espouse, pour mère, et pour reyne des noces, une dame de grant
lignage, qui en biauté, en bonté, en pureté, et en toute vertu surmon-
tast toutes les dames du monde. Et combien que les lisans cestui
traitié du mariage aient bien cognoissance de cest noble dame—et
benoîs seront tous ceulx & toutes celles qui bien la cognistront &
dévotement la suivont—et toutefois il ne nous doit pas amirer donyr
souvent recorder les graces et condicions de ceste poissant reyne
dont tant de bien est vénû à nostre génération.

Or entrons donques en la matère. Il fû jadis un noble baron en
Israhel, riche et poissant et doubtant Dieu, en dignité de prestre,
apellé Joachim. Et ot une compagne et espouse pareille à ses condicions, appellée Anne, laquelle estoit bréhaigne et ne portoit
point de fruit, dont il estoient à grant dolour. Et ainsi furent vingt
ans sans avoir lignée. Dont une fois Joachim, faisant son office en
tempre, et offrant sacrefice, fû rédargnés vilainement du Souverain
Evesque des Juifz, parcequ'il n'avoit engendré fruit en Israhel, disant
qu'il n'estoit pas dignes d'offrir à Dieu sacrifice. Dont Joachim se
parti, confus et deshonnoré, et s'en ala avec ses pasteurs et bestes
bien environ trente journées, pour fuîr la vergoingne, et Anne
démoura en Nazareth, confuse et toute honteuse.

Grant temps avoit passé qu'il avoient voué à Dieu que, si Dieu
leur donnoit fruit de lignié, il le présenteroient au service de Dieu.
Sìcommé, de ceste gracieuse estoire, le glorieux saint Jérome prolixe-
ment en traite, finablement, peut abrégrer nostre escripture; et
par l'annonciacion de l'angre faite à Joachim, et à Anne, Joachim
rétourna à son hostel, et Anne conçût la trèsdoulce Vièrge Marie,
laquelle fû saintifiée au ventre de sa mère plus, sans nulle comparison,
que ne fû onques nulle pure humaine créature; et fû reservée et
née pure, sainte, et nète, et a morti en lui le fomite, c'est l'aguillon,

de tout pechié, et véniel et mortel, ce que à autre créature pure ne fû onques otroié.

Quel merveille! car le créateur de toutes créatures singulièrement avoit crée cestui noble vaissiau pour recevoir et herbergier en lui le pain de vie, qui donne vie aux angres et aux hommes. C'estoit son propre corps, et en cestui vaissiau précieux, à grant merveille et joie nonpareille de nostre généracion, furent solempnelment célébrée les noces cy-dessus souvent répétées.

Que diray-je plus de nostre josne reyne, de sa biauté, de sa bonté, de ses vertus et graces à lui otroiées? Je ne souffis pas descripre souffisamment comme il appartendroit les vertus de la Reyne du Ciel. Car ma penne est trop maltaillé; et, si toute l'iaue de la mer estoit devenue encre, et tous les plains de Syrie estoient parchemin, et tout le bois de la forest de bière estoit devenu pennes à escripre, il ne souffisoient pas pour descripre ne desclairier la millesième de la millesième partie; ne tant par aucune comparisson, qui est nulz en qualité et en quantité, comme d'une toute seule goûte d'iaue à toute la mer ocayne. Je escripray donques, par la grâce, ce que je pouvray, non pas ce que je deveroye; et ay esperance en lui que, par sa doulce bonté, elle prendra nient ou paou pour bonne volenté.

Retournant à nostre matère. Quant la doulce pucelle et vièrge fu sévérée de la mamelle, et qu'elle ot trois ans, Joachim et Anne la présenterent au temple, acomplissant à Dieu leur veu. Et à la présentacion de la petite Vièrge Marie, de trois ans, à parlui et sans aucune aide humaine, monta les quinze degrés du temple, qui estoient et grans et haus, par telle manière et sì viguereusement, que le Souverain Evesque, et tous ceulx qui la virent, trop fort s'en merveillerent; qui estoit bien chose évident que la josne vièrge tendoit à Dieu.

Le père et la mère laisserent leur fille au service de Dieu, en la compaignie des vièrges filles des grans barons d'Israhel, qui estoient nouries au temple auquelle fû nostre josne reyne la doulce Vièrge Marie il appert, car les angres s'en esjoissoient. Et selonc ce que récite Saint Jérome, Marie de son propre mouvement, par grâce du Saint Esperit qui doulcement la gouvernoit, ordonna de sa vie en telle manière que, du matin jusques à l'eure de Tierce, elle se tenoit en oroison sans intermission, et, de l'eure de Tierce jusques à l'eure de nonne, elle labouroit de ses belles mains, faisans tissus de soie, et autres choses qui appartenoient au service de Dieu au temple.

Et de ce faire n'arestoit jusques atant que l'angre du ciel descendoit, et lui appartoit sa refeccion corporele. Et après sa refeccion elle retornoit tantost à l'oration et à ce qu'elle ne fausist aux euvres de misericorde. La viande qui lui estoit livrée chascun jour des évesques de la loy, elle donnoit pour Dieu, et ne mengoit autre chose que ce que l'angre lui aportoit.

Onques, selonc ce que dient Saint Ambroise et Saint Jeromie, elle ne fû trouvée vuiseuse ou elle lisoit et estudioit en la loy de Dieu, ou elle s'ocupoit en oracion ou contemplacion, ou lanoit les vestemens de l'office divin. Et toutes choses que les anciennes dames au temple ne pouoient faire, elle faisoit tréshumblement, et souvent reprenoit les autres vièrges, ses compaignes demourans au temple, quant elle les veoit ou trop rire, ou faire ou dire aucune chose deshonneste. Et briefment, selonc ce que dient les sains, dès qu'elle entra au temple, qu'elle n'avoit que trois ans, elle apparoit sì saige et sì menre comme s'elle eust esté en l'aage de trente ans.

Et combien que, en la loy d'escripture, malediction estoit offerte à chascun du peuple d'Israhel qui ne feroit fruit de ligne à Dieu par mariage, toutefois nostre doulce Vièrge Marie, saintement inspirée pour mieux plaire à Dieu, voua virginité, et fû primière qui onques le fiest.

Quel merveil, de car les angres la gouvernoient, et le Saint Esperit lui enseignoit la loy de Dieu et tout ce qu'elle avoit à faire, par telle manière qu'elle entendoit parfaitement l'escripture des prophètes. Et quant elle lisoit la prophésie d'Ysaye, de la vièrge qui devoit concevior Messias le Redemptour du monde, et les autres prophésies appartenans à la dicte vièrge, la doulce Vièrge Marie lors se trouvoit ausì comme ravie, et non sans larmes de dévotion, déprioit doulcement à Dieu qui li fiest grâce de tant vivre qu'elle peust veoir la dicte vièrge, et lui servir en lui lavant les pies. Et parceque Souveraine humilité regnoit en lui, elle n'eust osé pensser jamais ne ymaginer de lui mesmes, qu'elle fust celle vièrge promise en la loy par laquelle le monde devoit estre racheté.

Elle estoit toujiours la primière et la derrenière aux heures canoniques à pronouncier les siaumes de David, et les autres prophésies. Ne jamais nulz ne la viest rire, ne dire parôle vuiseuse. Et sans intermission elle beneissoit Dieu. Et afin que le nom de Dieu ne partist de sa bouche, quant on la saluoit, pour resalut " Deo gracias " elle respondoit. Quel mervielle, car les angres estoient si familier de lui que nuit et jour il estoient avec lui pour lui garder, servir, et honnourer. Onques telle vièrge ne fû, ne jamais ne sera; et très benoîs sera celui qui doulcement l'amera.

Il estoit de coustumme, au peuple de Dieu d'Israhel, que les filles des princes, barons, et seigneurs estoient nouries au temple jusques au temps qu'elles estoient en l'aage d'estre mariée, afin qu'elles fussent meiulz gardées. Et quant elles estoient prestes pour mariage, les Souverain Evesques de la loy les renvoiorent solempnelment à l'ostel de leurs parens. Or vint le temps que nostre Vièrges, tant de fois doulcement répété, ot treize ans et en l'aage d'estre mariée, et les autres vièrges ausi qui avoient esté nouries au temple avec lui, quant le Souverain Evesque ot donné sa sentence, que les vièrges retournassent à leurs parens, pour estre mariées, la doulce Vièrge Marie seule respondi, que ce elle ne pouvoit faire, et pour deux causes: l'une, parceque son père et sa mère l'avoient vouée à Dieu à toujiours mais, pour estre à son service; l'autre, parcequ'elle avoit voué virginité, et s'estoit dédiée au service de Dieu.

Quant le Souverain Evesque ouy ainsì parler la doulce Vièrge Marie, il fû tout esbahi, et ne sot que respondre à la vièrge, doubtant d'aler contre l'escriture du prophète David, qui dit, "Voues à Dieu, et à Dieu rendez vos veus"; d'autre part, il doubtoit à entroduire un nouvelle coustume en la loy de Moyses, c'est à savoir, que les filles demourassent vierges, sans porter fruit, ne acroistre le peuple de Deiu; et sur cest doubte, il ot conseil aux anciens de la loy, et fû determiné que, sur un tel fait de nouvelleté, il estoit expedient de requerre le conseil de Dieu, qui, par une voix du ciel, manda que la dicte vièrge fust mariée et baillie en garde à Joseph, le viellart, qui estoit de droite lignié issus de la lignié de David, sìcomme par l'estoire publique appert; et de la verge de Joseph, qui flori, et du coulon qui vint dessus, et des autres mistères et miracles qui avindrent touchant à la matère, lesquelz je trespasse, pour cause de briefté, et parcequ'elles sont asses communes.

La doulce Vièrge Marie, comme dit est, fû conjointe, par sacrament de mariage espirituel, au saint viellart Joseph vierge. Et fû sa vraie espouse selonc la loy, demourant vièrge, et aussi Joseph vièrge demoura son vray espous, faite l'aliance susdicte au temple. Joseph s'en ala en Bethleem, sa cité, c'est-à-dire dont il estoit; car il estoit de la maignie et lignie de David, qui fû de Bethleem, pour appareillier tout ce qui faisoit besoing pour les noces de lui et de Marie, à certain temps célébrer. Et la très sainte et esleue vièrge de Dieu Marie acompaignié de septes autres vièrges, que le Souverain Evesque lui bailla pour lui acompaigner, lesquelles avoient este nouries avec lui au tempre, s'en ala hastivement devers ses parens en Nazareth dont elle estoit née.

Et ne fait pas à oublier, pour nostre consolacion, c'est-à-savoir que, quant la doulce et tendre Vièrge Marie fû sur son partie du temple, et les septes vièrges avec lui, comme dit est, les dictes vièrges avecques Marie furent d'acord de fair un sort, par manière debatement gracieux, pour veoir, par le sort et volenté de Dieu, laquelle de toutes les vièrges susdites seroit chevetaine d'elles au chemin, pour avoir le gouvernement des autres, et, par aventure, pour non donner travail à nostre doulce Marie, qui estoit tendre de corps, et n'avoit pas apriz d'aler à pie, ne de fort traveillier.

Les vièrges, lors, mistrent en sort septes jonèles, sicomme touaillons, de laine et de soie, de diverses coulours, entre lesquelz avoit une pièce de drap de soie vermeille, qui s'appelle pourpre, et fû dit, de commun accord des vièrges, que celle qui, par le sort, averoit la pourpre, seroit leur reyne. Et briefment, quant ce vint au prendre, la pourpre eschei d'aventure, mais par l'ordonnance divine, à la doulce Vièrge Marie.

Lors les vièrges de là en avant appelèrent Marie leur reyne. Et de là primièrement, elle prist le nom d'estre appellée Reyne des Vièrges. Et selonc l'estoire de ceste gracieuse matère, l'angre s'apparu entre elles, et confourma le nom de "Reyne des Vièrges," du cîel, et de la terre, à la doulce Vièrge Marie.

Appendices
Bibliography
Acknowledgments

Appendix I

The text of the *Salve Regina* is taken from Clemens Blume and Guido Maria Dreves, *Hymnographi Latini*, p. 318 (*Analecta Hymnica*, vol. 50 [Leipzig, O. R. Reisland, 1905–1907]). My translation follows.

Salve, regina misericordiae,
Vita, dulcedo et spes nostra, salve!
Ad te clamamus exsules filii Evae,
Ad te suspiramus gementes et flentes
In hac lacrimarum vale.
Eia ergo, advocata nostra,
Illos tuos misericordes oculos ad nos converte
Et Iesum, benedictum fructum ventris tui,
Nobis post hoc exsilium ostende,
O clemens, O pia,
O dulcis Maria.

Hail, O queen of mercy,
Our life, sweetness, and hope, hail!
To you we cry, the banished sons of Eve,
To you we sigh, sobbing and weeping,
In this valley of tears.
Quickly then, our advocate,
Turn to us those eyes of your mercy
And show us, after this exile,
Jesus, the blessed fruit of your womb,
O kind, O pious,
O sweet Mary.

Appendix II

The text of *Veni creator spiritus* is taken from Clemens Blume and Guido Maria Dreves, *Hymnographi Latini*, p. 193 (*Analecta Hymnica*, vol. 50 [Leipzig, O. R. Reisland, 1905–1907]). My translation follows.

Veni creator, spiritus,
Mentes tuorum visita,
Imple superna gratia,
Quae tu creasti pectora.

Qui paracletus diceris
Donum Dei altissimi,
Fons vivus, ignis, caritas
Et spiritalis unctio.

Tu septiformis munere,
Dextrae Dei tu digitus,
Tu rite promisso patris
Sermone ditans guttura.

Accende lumen sensibus,
Infunde amorem cordibus,
Infirma nostri corporis
Virtute firmans perpeti.

Hostem repellas longius
Pacemque dones protinus,
Ductore sic te praevio
Vitemus omne noxium.

Per te sciamus, da, patrem
Noscamus utque filium,
Te utriusque spiritum
Credamus omni tempore.

Praesta, pater piisime
Patrique compar unice
Cum spiritu paraclito
Regnans per omne saeculum.

Come, Creator, Spirit;
Visit the minds of your own,
Fill with grace from above
The breast of him you created.

You who are called Paraclete,
The gift of the highest God,
Living fountain, fire, charity
And spiritual anointing.

You are the gift in seven forms,
You, the finger of God's right hand,
You, the just promise of the Father,
Enriching our throats with words.

Light up the light of our senses,
Infuse love in our hearts,
And our weak bodies
Make firm with enduring strength.

Drive our enemy far away,
And give us present peace,
So that with you as our leader,
We may avoid all peril.

Allow us to know, through you, the Father,
And to know the Son,
And let us believe through all time
In you, the Spirit of both.

Be present, most merciful Father,
And the unique equal of the Father,
With the Comforter Spirit
Reigning through all ages.

Bibliography

Bell, Dora M. *Étude sur Le songe du vieil pèlerin de Philippe de Mézières 1327–1405.* Geneva: Droz, 1955.

Coopland, George W. *Le Songe du Vieil Pèlerin of Philippe de Mézières, Chancellor of Cyprus.* 2 vols. Cambridge: Cambridge University Press, 1969.

Frank, Grace. "The authorship of Le mystère de Griseldis." *Modern Language Notes* 51 (1936):217–222.

Jorga, Nicholas. *Philippe de Mézières, 1327–1405, et la Croisade au XIVe siècle.* Bibliothèque de l'École des Hautes Études, no. 109. Paris, 1896.

Kishpaugh, Sister M. Jerome. *The Feast of the Presentation of the Virgin Mary in the Temple: An Historical and Literary Study.* Washington, D.C.: Catholic University Press, 1941.

La Piana, George. "The Byzantine Iconography of the Presentation of the Virgin Mary to the Temple and a Latin Religious Pageant." In *Late Classical and Mediaeval Studies in Honor of Albert Mathias Friend, Jr.,* ed. Kurt Weitzmann, pp. 261–271. Princeton, N.J.: Princeton University Press, 1955.

Weiner, Albert. *Philippe de Mézières' Description of the Dramatic Office for the Feast of the Presentation of the Virgin Mary in the Temple.* Translated, with an introduction on "The Rise of Modern Acting." New Haven: Andrew Kner, 1958.

Young, Karl. "Philippe de Mézières' Dramatic Office for the Presentation of the Virgin." *PMLA* 26 (1911):181–234.

————. *The Drama of the Medieval Church.* 2 vols. Oxford: Clarendon Press, 1933.

Acknowledgments

I wish to thank the Documents Division of the Bibliothèque Nationale for supplying me with microfilm of MS fr. 1175. I wish also to thank the Research Councils of the University of Nebraska and of the University of California at Berkeley for funds and assistance.

R. S. H.